I've Never Met A Dead Person I Didn't Like

Initiation by Spirits

I've Never Met
A Dead Person
I Didn't Like

Initiation by Spirits

Sherrie Dillard

Winchester, UK
Washington, USA

JOHN HUNT PUBLISHING

First published by Sixth Books, 2019
Sixth Books is an imprint of John Hunt Publishing Ltd., No. 3 East St., Alresford,
Hampshire SO24 9EE, UK
office@jhpbooks.com
www.johnhuntpublishing.com
www.6th-books.com

For distributor details and how to order please visit the 'Ordering' section on our website.

Design: Stuart Davies

UK: Printed and bound by CPI Group (UK) Ltd, Croydon, CR0 4YY
US: Printed and bound by Thomson-Shore, 7300 West Joy Road, Dexter, MI 48130

The people and events described in this book are all true. However, some of the names and
identifying details of those discussed have been changed. Any resemblances, resulting from
these changes, is entirely coincidental and unintentional.

We operate a distinctive and ethical publishing philosophy in
all areas of our business, from our global network of authors to
production and worldwide distribution.

Contents

Acknowledgments

Thank you to the fantastic committed team at 6th Books. In particular John Hunt for his kind words, Dominic C. James, Elizabeth Radley for her streamline editing, Beccy Conway, Maria Barry, Mary Flatt, Stuart Davies, Nick Welch, Trevor Greenfield and Krystina Kellingley. Special thank you to Gavin Lee Davies for his enthusiasm. It's a wonderful blessing to be able to be a part of this innovative and creative enterprise.

I would also like to acknowledge my sister, Sandee Washington, for her encouragement, and my children, Aiden and Mariah, for bursting into my life and making it all seem so normal.

To the spirit guides, angels, Mother Mary and other enlightened beings who have always been by my side, and taught me to be me and to love myself. Much gratitude for pushing me to write this book. I know I've not always been the easiest student.

This book is Yours.

Part I Raised By Spirits

Chapter 1

To Heaven and Back

Most days are the same for me. For the past thirty years I've sat in my office with the sun pouring through the window and talked to the living and the dead. By outer standards my day-to-day life may seem boring or even conventional: work, walk the dogs, eat and sleep. Yet, my real life is lived in the wonder and richness of the spirit realm. Most days I talk to more dead people than I do people alive in the physical world and this is fine with me. I've never met a dead person I didn't like. Even those who have been lousy parents, drug addicts, mean drunks or self-centered and cared only about themselves. Once they are dead, the flimsy illusions fall away. They wake to a more beautiful and loving self than they ever imagined.

From my vantage point as a medium I regularly witness heartfelt connections and the generous healing love of spirit. The dead have a lot to say to those they watch over and the family and friends they left behind, and I feel fortunate they trust me to help them say it.

The Remembering

For as long as I can remember I have been able to see and talk to spirits. When I was seven months old I had a near death experience and made a brief visit to the other side. When I stopped breathing and turned blue my mother called the fire department. On the way to the hospital, a fireman revived me. According to my mother, I was not breathing for what seemed like a long time and she was sure that I was gone for good.

I never thought much about what happened until I started giving professional readings. My first office space was on the ground floor of a rather plain-looking office building. When

Marcella, the unofficial divine mother of the area, invited me to share an office space with her, I jumped at the opportunity. Marcella used the larger of the two rooms, while I had the smaller one. Before we rented the space, my office was likely used as a closet. It had no windows and I could barely get two chairs and a small aquarium in it, which at the time seemed essential. Marcella had been in the new-age healing business for a long time and I felt fortunate to be able to share the space with her.

One afternoon Marcella saw me leaning over a sink in the ladies bathroom gasping for air. As far back as I could remember this had been a problem. Sometimes my throat would tighten and constrict while I ate or if I was stressed. However, this was also equally likely to occur for no apparent reason. I never knew why or when this might happen and could go for a long period of time breathing normally, and then seemingly out of nowhere, I would find myself struggling for air.

As uncomfortable as these episodes could be, I never lost consciousness or felt as if I was in serious danger. My breath always came back to me. Doctors couldn't find anything wrong and over time I became accustomed to the odd intervals of wheezing and feeling my throat close up.

When Marcella saw me hunched over and gasping for air she looked concerned. Placing her warm hand on my back, she waited for my breath to come back.

After I explained to her that I was fine and that this happened every now and then, she seemed eager to help.

"I think we need to do some breath work," she said. "This is most likely caused by some kind of energy blockage, probably an emotional issue."

With as much as I knew about energy and the chaos of my past, I didn't doubt that this was true. I always knew that there was likely something motivating these episodes that I might want to investigate.

"We can release and heal whatever it is that is causing this distress. You can't let this go on," she said.

The next afternoon, I lay on a soft bed in Marcella's dimly-lit office. Seated by my side, she told me to close my eyes.

"Breathe deeply," she said. "I'll breathe with you."

Her deep inhales and exhales seemed a little overly dramatic. However, my breath fell in unison with hers. As I continued to breathe, a wave of heat moved through me starting at my toes and I tossed aside the blanket that lay on top of me. Marcella had her hand on my arm and it felt odd as I wasn't used to this kind of caring attention.

Inhaling, I smelled an herbal aroma coming from the aromatherapy diffuser. I tried to identify the scent, but couldn't. The sweet and nutty smell was probably a homemade mixture. I was thankful that it wasn't sandalwood which can be highly overused in these kinds of situations. Realizing that my preoccupation with determining the scent was keeping me from deeper relaxation, I went back to focusing on my breath.

With this my thoughts began to become more distant. The low lights and subtle new-age instrumental music that faintly played in the background gently rocked me into relaxation. I had to hand it to Marcella, she knew how to set the scene; I couldn't resist the pulling inward and my conscious mind began to softly drift.

Slowly inner movement, like the barely audible sounds of distant rumbling thunder, started to awaken from deep within. A faint glimmer of dormant awareness, something within me buried away, wanted my attention. A force was being dislodged and as it became stronger it took on a life of its own. I knew that I could no longer hide from it. At the same time I tried to listen and follow Marcella's instructions, as she began to breathe short sharp breaths.

"Breathe with me, fast breaths," she said.

Lying on her bed with her arm on my shoulder, I fully trusted Marcella. She had a vast array of healing modalities and

4

techniques at her disposal. I knew she wanted to help me and I was grateful to her for this.

However, as I continued to breathe short breaths, I questioned my decision to go through this process. Beginning to feel the uncomfortable sensation of my throat tightening and panic creeping up from an unknown inner hiding place, I wanted to either run away as fast as I could or nonchalantly go to lunch as if none of this was happening.

Instead, I felt a rolling storm of sadness, terror and grief well up within me. It was powerful and I knew I couldn't control it. As it gained momentum my body started to quiver, then shake, and the slight nudge of inner alarm, that I often heard and felt but continually pushed back, came rushing forward with a force that could not be denied. A moment later the intensity of the grief reached my mind and heart and I began to cry. This was not a polite whimper, but a messy nose running, help me get the hell out of here kind of sobbing.

Along with the intensity of emotions, I began to feel surging sensations in my body and see images. Some of what I saw and felt appeared in fragments and quick and repetitive scenes that I simultaneously felt and knew the meaning of. Over and over the images, feelings and thoughts emerged until I couldn't deny what I was simultaneously witnessing and experiencing. Still I couldn't accept it and I didn't want to acknowledge what had happened so long ago. Like the waves of the ocean driven by a storm, wave after wave of awareness, emotion, sensation and resistance moved through me. Until finally the truth took a defiant stance and I let the illusions fall away.

"She wouldn't do this," I said, while squirming on the bed and gasping for air. "No, no, no, she wouldn't do this," I kept repeating.

"Who wouldn't do what?" Marcella asked.

I didn't want to ever answer her. I wanted to forget all of this, sit up, leave and get on with my day. Yet despite my denial, the scene continued to unfold and it revealed layer after layer of fear and sadness.

Trembling and weak, I felt the past trauma and at the same time I watched it from a bird's eye view. As the pressure of a pillow was clamped tight down on me, I squirmed and struggled. I saw myself, a little speck of a being, fighting and I felt the will to survive. The pillow was bigger than I was, and as hard as I tried I couldn't breathe.

I was overwhelmed with the awareness that I was being suffocated. Still I refused to accept what was happening. Yet this long-buried memory from the past was too strong. Denying this truth was like trying to hold back a tornado and at the same time ignore that it was ripping through your home and destroying everything in its path. My soul was being torn apart by an inescapable force, and I couldn't breathe and get away. The raw abscess of my past had just revealed itself and demanded acknowledgment.

"What's happening? Tell me what is happening," Marcella again asked me.

I didn't want to tell her and I couldn't breathe or talk, anyway. Then all of a sudden, I felt myself surrender and give up and everything changed.

I was no longer fighting a losing battle, it was over. I was someplace different where it was still and peaceful. I was hiding behind a lady, a very tall lady, with a blue and gold dress on. I was trying to stay as quiet as possible, because I didn't want her to notice me. She was familiar and I felt warm and safe with her and I wanted to stay with her. However, as quiet and hidden as I tried to be, I knew that she was aware of me.

"I will be really good. No one will notice me," I told her.

I desperately wanted to stay with her. She never spoke a word, but I knew that I had to go back.

"Please anything else," I pleaded with her. "Let me be here with you..."

Then I saw the dim and fading outline of a man and I knew that he was a fireman. I could smell his sweat and his breath. It wasn't unpleasant, just strong and I felt that he wanted to help me.

All of a sudden, Marcella touched my shoulder and I was back on the bed.

"Sherrie, what's happening?" she asked.

I told her about the tall lady and the fireman, and I lay there quietly. As the images, sensations and feelings stated to fade, I felt dizzy and empty.

"This really sucks," I thought. "Where are the angels, spirit guides and light beings that I have come to rely on? Shouldn't they be helping me right about now, and coming to my aid?"

Hopeful that a loving and wise spirit influence would come forward to soothe me and disperse the unrelenting revelations and pain that coursed through my mind, heart and body, I sent out an SOS to the spirit realm. Immediately, I felt the presence of one of my spirit guides. Unlike the warm and comforting energy of some of my guides, this spirit was a bit detached and a more say-it-like-it-is kind of guide.

Wanting to be comforted, I waited in expectation, but no warmth came my way.

Instead I received the intuitive message that, "It is your choice to suffer."

Surprised and confused, this message pissed me off.

"Oh, really, this is my choice to be suffocated as an infant," I thought.

Then another message, "You chose your family for the opportunities that they offered; the lessons are important."

I wasn't in the mood to hear this and decided to talk to Marcella instead. Slowly I opened my eyes still wet with tears and sweat. Looking down at me, she had a somewhat bewildered expression. There was a blanket rolled into a ball near my head, and as I moved, a few strands of its yellow yarn landed on my face. New-age music continued its constant soothing, but useless, beat in the background.

Still not wanting to talk about what just happened, I said nothing. Marcella in her gentle voice asked, "How are you?"

"My mother wouldn't suffocate me," I said.

"Do you think that maybe it feels that this could have happened, but it really didn't."

I looked at Marcella and she looked at me. Snotty nosed, still in denial and defending my mother against the cruel raw truth, I thought, "You have got to be kidding. This isn't something that I made up."

We both knew the truth, but neither of us was willing to go any further with it at that time.

Chapter 2

Early Visits from the Other Side

The daughter of a Northern Italian immigrant, my mother had three older brothers and grew up in Queens in New York City. Both musicians, her parents met while playing music at a wedding. Her mother played piano and her father the violin.

My mother's upbringing taught her how to politely drink martinis in the afternoon and to dress for dinner. In stark contrast my father grew up in a lumber mill town in New Hampshire, close to the Canadian border. After high school he joined the army, and while on leave in Florida one summer, he met my mother who was there vacationing with a friend.

Enamored by the vast expanse of sandy beaches, my mother changed her name from Amabel to Sandy that summer. Until the end of her life this is what she was called. After a brief courtship, she married my father and he finished his time in the service.

During the first year of their marriage my older sister Sandee was born. A few months later my mother became pregnant again. When it came time to deliver the baby, she knew something was wrong. As hard as she tried she couldn't push her out. Upon closer examination the doctor became alarmed and summoned help from a specialist. A few hours later they discovered that the baby had an open spine and was hydrocephalic.

My father chain-smoking and pacing in the delivery room was worried. The birth was taking longer than expected. As he watched doctors and nurses go in and out of the delivery room he waited for news, but none came. Eventually, a doctor with a concerned look on his face and not the happy smile my father had been expecting sought him out. He explained that there was a problem and that my father needed to decide whether or not to try and save the baby or my mother, as only one of them could survive the birth.

However, in my father's version of this event, he dismissed the idea that there was ever a choice.

"The doctor needed my consent to go forward with a necessary procedure," he said. "Before I was asked to make a decision I told the doctor to save my wife."

My father didn't share much else and it never seemed like he wanted to talk about it.

They named the baby Dawn Marie and a month after she passed back into the light of the other side, my mother was pregnant again.

Not aware that she had lost the baby, people who she encountered while out and about at places like the bank and grocery store would stop her and ask, "Are you still pregnant?" or "Is that baby ever going to be born?"

Her due date was close to my father's birthday and my mother drank castor oil to induce labor and have the baby born early. She wanted a special birthday gift for my father, and after an easy labor, I was born. My mother told me that after the tragic loss of Dawn Marie, it was like the baby Jesus himself had arrived. I don't think my mother ever loved me more than at my birth. Whatever Jesus similarity she saw in me was short-lived. Two years later my brother was born, and two years after this, she brought home another brother.

I am not sure what came first, being told that I had a sister in heaven or seeing her blond curly hair and angelic face, and feeling her presence as soft light. Like a sibling who gets to go to Disneyland or an exotic and exciting destination, I thought that Dawn Marie was lucky to be in heaven. She got to be with us whenever she wanted, but was spared the cold weather, baloney sandwiches and the chaos in my home. She was happy and peaceful and I didn't know anyone else who felt this way. I relied on her as you would a big sister and called on her in times of need. Usually I pleaded with her to help calm my mother down. Prone to unexpected outbursts that often included yelling, throwing things and slapping, hitting or pushing, it seemed to me that only unseen intervention could stop her.

The Loved Spirits

My mother seldom spoke of her family, unless they were dead. Those on the other side were more loving, cherished and closer to her than the living. Despite the grief my mother expressed when she talked about those who had passed over, she was soft and warm when she spoke of them. As she gazed into open space recalling her dead, I looked with her and often saw and felt the spirits she spoke of. The dead were good, the living not so much.

My mother's favorite dead person was her mother. The stories of how Dawn Marie and my grandmother passed over were told and retold. Yet every time the raw sting of their deaths hung in the air like it had just happened.

The story of my grandmother's passing always began with a recounting of how her father left her for another woman when my mother was a teenager. Not long after my mother and grandmother moved into an apartment together, she collapsed and died of a heart attack while my mother was in the bathroom getting ready for church. My mother believed that my grandmother died of a broken heart.

"My father betrayed her, that's what killed her," she said.

The loved dead also included Matty, her favorite brother. A fireman, he died at a young age from an injury he sustained while fighting a fire. His fireman's hat was kept in our hall coat closet, almost as if one day he would come in and ask for it.

There was also Aunt Mary-Ann, my mother's best friend since childhood who was like a sister to her. After my grandmother's death my mother moved into Aunt Mary-Ann's home where she stayed until she graduated from high school.

When she came to visit, my mother was more relaxed and even a bit playful. One morning during breakfast while stirring her coffee, my mother said, "Aunt Mary-Ann died last night. She was sick."

Then she got up and went to her room, shut the door and didn't come out for a few days. It took awhile for her to mention Aunt Mary-Ann again. When my mother did talk about her I could see and feel Aunt Mary-Ann's spirit standing next to her. Tall and thin and with a big smile just like she had when she was living, I looked forward to her visits.

My Grandfather Alive and Dead

Unlike the spirits who visited often, my grandfather came to our home once. I was ten years old and the preparation for his visit had us all sleepless and nervous. My mother acted like the King and his entourage had consented to visit the peasants. In the neighborhood where I grew up, everyone knew everyone else's business. Most of my friends came from large French Canadian, Italian and Irish families. Any time of day or night they might have a relative stop by and on the weekends there was usually a family celebration of some kind happening somewhere in the neighborhood.

We were not like the other families. We didn't have any cousins, grandmothers and grandfathers, uncles and aunts stopping by. The visit from my grandfather was big news that had us anxious with anticipation.

On the day of his visit, my brothers, my sister and I anxiously looked out the big window in our living room and waited for him. When we spotted a new-looking black car turn down our street, we knew this had to be him. Everyone in the neighborhood drove junky cars. With the snow and salted roads in the winter and large families with working-class paychecks, most of the bottom halves of the cars were either covered with rust or chunks of it had rusted off.

When the car came to a stop in our driveway, we ran around in circles yelling, "He's here, he's here." Then ran out to meet him.

In keeping with his distinguished-looking car, my grandfather slowly opened the door and stepped out wearing a black suit and shiny black shoes. Years later, while watching the movie, *The Godfather*, I was struck with the similarities between him and the style and attitude of the gangsters. My grandfather casually surveyed the toy-strewn lawn of dead grass and weeds and the tall electrical tower in our backyard and didn't seem too excited.

We all stood there for a few minutes looking at each other like we had just encountered alien visitors. As my mother introduced my sister, myself and my two brothers, my grandfather looked each one of us up and down and nodded his head. There were no hugs and warm embraces. Flanked by one of my uncles who also wore a black suit, we solemnly made our way into the house. As my grandfather sat in one of our wobbly kitchen chairs, I studied him. Watching every move he made, I searched for any similarities between him and my mother. He had brown sunspots on his white hands and the same color of eyes and large mouth as my mother.

As we gathered around the table the stress began to take a toll on me. The emotional tension was thick and heavy and I could feel how much this visit meant to my mother. She wanted her father's love and approval, and I desperately wanted him to hug her or say a kind word. I focused on this thought and stared at him in the hope that I could plant this idea in his mind and heart. Maybe this would help to dissolve the bitter anger and hatred that she had for him. Unfortunately my powers of persuasion were not as strong as I had hoped. I just started to feel weak and overwhelmed.

While I stuffed myself with the cheese and fruit that my mother had arranged on glass dishes which I had never before seen, the awkward silence and strained conversation continued. As I moved on to some fancy-looking cookies, my mother asked my sister to play her accordion. Never one to shy away from an audience, she strapped on the large red and black shiny instrument and confidently moved her hands up and down the keys pumping out a familiar song. I watched my grandfather's face, hopeful that a little smile would escape. Instead he remained expressionless, until she finished.

"Now, I'll show you the right way to play that song," he said.

At this, the room became quiet. We all knew that my sister was a musical genius, at least, we believed her to be. She was a member of the accordion band in another town, no small honor.

My mother's expression immediately changed. The "I want to make you happy" sounding voice was gone. In its place was the stern smile and fake-sounding laugh that meant trouble. Although she was not in the best mood to begin with, there had been at least hope, but no longer.

She had brought out the dishes with the painted but fading green leaves that we only used on special occasions. The house was clean top to bottom, we were all dressed in our church clothes and my sister had done her best to entertain and impress. Now, my mother was done playing nice. The family reunion was over and my grandfather left as cold and distant as he arrived.

Years later my mother still mocked her father who had the audacity to tell my sister how to play the accordion.

"Like Mr. Know-it-all," she said. "Didn't smile or appreciate anything, just sat in his chair motionless, judging me as if he is so much better."

Another Visit

I never saw my grandfather again, not in the physical body, anyway. Years later after he died, he appeared to me and insisted I give my mother a message. For a few weeks I woke to him standing at the foot of my bed. Similar to when I first met him, he had brown spots on his hands and his eyes looked like my mother's. I was initially surprised by his presence and wanted to ignore him. Most spirits were warm and friendly or didn't pay me much attention. Not him, he just stood there and stared at me. Morning after morning just after waking, he appeared to me and I wondered if he would ever leave me alone.

Finally one morning, after burying my head in my pillow hoping that he would go away, I sat up and asked him, "What do you want?"

His message was clear and consistent.

"Please tell your mother that I am sorry and that I love her."

I was not thrilled about this request. As much as I wanted my mother to know that her father loved her, she became bat-shit crazy when her father was mentioned. I learned long ago not to ask questions about her past. I told my grandfather that I didn't want to tell her this and even if I did she wouldn't believe me. Still, he wouldn't give up. Just wanting this to be over, I told him that I would give her the message, but that he had to help. I don't know what I expected him to do, but he was so good at getting my attention I knew he could figure something out.

For several days I said nothing and waited for the right opportunity. Walking into the kitchen one morning, I saw my mother sitting quietly and looking out the window. This was a rare moment of quiet that I knew I had to take advantage of.

"Maybe your father is sorry and he loves you," I said.

Then I stood stiff and silent and waited for all hell to break loose. There was no way that I was going to tell her that her father wouldn't leave me alone until I told her this. If she didn't accept the message, I didn't want her to be angry at me for talking to him, or more likely, to think that I made the whole thing up.

To my surprise, she continued looking out the window.

Without looking at me, almost as if she was speaking to the air, she said, "The first winter I lived with my mother my father bought me a beautiful coat that I loved. Maybe he did love me in his own way."

Although her response seemed odd, it was nothing short of a miracle. Not wanting to press my luck I slowly crept out of the room.

On my way down the hall I sent a silent message to my grandfather, "Maybe you're not so bad after all. Thanks for anything you did to help her feel your love and not want to kill me."

My Grandmother Gives a Command

I came to know my mother's mother in a similar way. Although she passed over long before my birth, she was a constant presence in my home when I was young. However, she was not like the other spirits who were often funny and talkative. She was quiet and I never knew if she was aware of me. Always close to my mother, she had a serious and concerned look on her face, like she was watching everything that my mother did. My spirit grandmother followed my mother around the house and didn't seem to notice anyone else.

Years later, I was surprised when she paid me a visit. Unlike my childhood when she was quiet and distant, she was determined to get my attention. It was a warm and sunny day and I lay on my bed depressed and just wanting to sleep. I was married at the time and we were having problems. I was numb and tired, always tired.

In one of the few times that I felt physical contact with a spirit, something gave me a good strong nudge and then did it again. Startled, I sat up and looked around the room. Near the door I saw the faint image of a woman and I knew it was her.

With a force that couldn't be denied, she said, "Get up right now and go tell your husband how you feel."

As she said this I felt the depression that she herself had lived with. Even though I saw her many times, this was the first time I felt a connection with her and that she was looking out for me.

For several years my husband and I had gone to marriage counseling off and on. Nothing seemed to be helping and I didn't know what to do.

"Get up and speak your truth," she said. "Come on, now."

My grandmother's message left no room for doubt and indecision. So I simply did what I was told. I got up from my bed, found my husband who was outside sitting in a lawn chair and started to talk.

Chapter 3

Dark Family Spirits

Although I was born on my father's birthday, I never felt the kind of special bond with him that I wanted and expected would one day happen. My father, who was named Benjamin Franklin, liked to tell stories about growing up poor. One of his favorites was how he and his five brothers regularly fought over the one bike they owned that didn't even have tires.

In the small New Hampshire town where he was raised there was a foul-smelling black suet powder from the logging mills that covered everything. When we went to visit his family we knew we were close when we saw a black cloud rising from a valley in the otherwise beautiful mountains.

Across from the three-story, three-family home where he spent his childhood, there was a lumber mill. At a young age he went to work there and ended up losing two fingers and mangling another. He liked to stick one of his finger stubs up his nose to make it appear as if his whole finger was up there. We always laughed hilariously when he did this.

With friends or out in public we would say, "Dad, put your finger up your nose, please, please."

More often than not, he would.

It was easy being with my father, he loved to make us laugh, sing to the cat and take naps. However, once we went to bed, his easygoing ways often took a turn for the worse. My father liked to drink. Although he looked like a bona fide businessman when he went to work, his large briefcase was actually a minibar. When opened, it revealed full-size liquor bottles, glasses and whatever else might be needed to mix a few drinks. My father was not a pleasant drunk. When he kissed me goodnight and I smelled whiskey on his breath, I knew that it would likely be a long night.

Although it was not uncommon for my parents to yell and argue during the day, they mostly saved the rougher stuff for the dark of night. However, my father once chased my mother down the street with a broom in broad daylight. Waking to the sound of things hitting the wall or my parents' shrieks and raised voices at night was not unusual.

One night, my sister and I woke up to the more ominous than normal sound of something crashing down on the floor. This was followed by silence, then more pounding on the walls and yelling that felt thick with anger. A dark slimy-like fear came over me and I didn't know what to do. My parents' voices were sharp and desperate in tone. After a high-pitched screech and the sound of my mother screaming and crying, we instinctually ran out of our bedroom not knowing what to expect. From the bathroom door, we heard my mother crying. While my sister pleaded with her to let her in, I went in search of my father. As I made my way through the house most of what was normally on a bookcase and end tables was on the floor. A lamp lay in pieces and I had to tiptoe over shards of glass from a broken light bulb. Next to one of my mother's hardcover books spread open on the floor, I noticed the little ceramic boy figurine that I was not allowed to touch. He wore green pants and held a large candle. His innocence bothered me and I wanted to step on him and crack him, even shatter him into little sharp pieces. Instead, I heard my father mumbling to himself from his bedroom and I went and stood in the doorway. Not allowed in my parents' room, he didn't seem to notice me standing at the door. As he wiped blood from his face, I noticed that his white tee shirt was torn and blotted with red splotches of blood and there were scratches on his arms and face. In the background, I still heard my sister trying to get my mother to come out of the bathroom. When she finally did, my mother strode through the house trying to act normal and I thought that we might get in trouble for being out of bed. Her eyes were swollen and her face was red with black streaks of mascara dripping down her cheeks, but there was no explanation.

"Go back to bed, girls, now," she said.

This was not the time to test her, so we silently walked back to our room. We had bunk beds and I was at the top. We didn't have a ladder and I just went up the back. Usually a pretty easy climb, but that night my body didn't seem to be able to do this the right way. Weak and trembling, I felt like I wasn't in my body and I just wanted to lie on the floor. Once I clumsily made it to bed, I closed my eyes and imagined that I could curl up into a little ball and lift up and go away. When I did this the sadness and heaviness became more distant. I could feel a space like a spiral seashell in the air above my bed that I could snuggle into. My sister Dawn Marie was there with me and it felt safe and warm. Smiling at me, she told me that it would all be okay.

"Go to sleep, you're safe," she said.

My body trembled and my eyes were wet with tears, but I knew I wasn't alone.

Swinging In the Sky

When I was six, my father left. It was a warm summer day and I was playing in the backyard with friends from the neighborhood. We were running around spraying each other with the hose and playing on the swing set. I was testing how high I could swing while being simultaneously sprayed with water. At the top of the swing arch with the sun and blue sky beaming down on me, I saw my father walk out of the side door of the house. I immediately jumped off the swing and went running to him.

Dripping wet and out of breath, I asked him, "Where're you going?"

He seemed distracted. "I have to do a few things," he said.

"Can I go with you?"

The obvious argument would have been that I was wearing

a bathing suit, muddy and wet. However, this went unnoticed.

Looking out toward the street, he said, "You can't come."

Something was going on. I could feel it. Despite the sunny day and the laughter and shouts not too far from me, my stomach tightened and tears came to my eyes.

"Please, can I come, please?" I asked.

My pleading seemed to wake him out of a daze. Looking down at me, our eyes met and I saw sadness and knew that something significant was happening. A feeling of sharpness and tightness came over me. I wanted to run, cry or plead with him, but all I did was stand there.

"Go play," was all he said.

A salesman for Esso Oil my father traveled quite a bit. In the back seat of his company car sat the mascot, a big ceramic tiger. Although I was dripping wet, the hot tar of the driveway started to burn my feet. I stood there anyway, immobile and watched my father and the back of the tiger's head drive down the street. He didn't come home that night, or the next or the next.

One evening about a week later, my mother made pancakes and bacon for dinner. While my youngest brother pawed me with his sticky syrupy hands, my mother causally said, "Your father isn't going to be living here any longer."

I felt a lump in my throat and I gasped for breath, but I wasn't surprised and sat in silence. My sister and brothers took the news hard and burst out crying. For me, he had already left and this just confirmed what I already knew.

Dark Spots

After the divorce we didn't see much of my father. He got married soon after he left and moved an hour or so away to be with his new wife and stepsons. They lived in a mobile home which we visited one time. While I played in their small yard I heard his wife yell at him through an open window.

"Take them home. This house is too small for four more

children," she said.

We soon piled into the car and never went back.

Every so often my father picked us up and took us to our aunt's mobile home. It was small and cluttered with figurines and cloudy with cigarette smoke. My father and aunt sat at a small kitchen table and drank and tried to speak in hushed voices. However, once they had a few drinks, the conversation got more animated with shrills of laughter, swearing and at times a few tears. We sat on the couch and did nothing.

In my aunt's bathroom there was a stack of nudie magazines, and my siblings and I found every excuse possible to continually go in and out of it and look at them. My father liked anything that had a naked woman on it. He had pens with pictures of women in bikinis in them. When you turned them upside down the women's bathing suit tops would come off. There was also a stack of playing cards that had a different nude woman on each card and the glass that he liked to drink whiskey from was shaped in the form of a woman's breasts. My mother would have been mad about all of this, so we never said anything to her.

Visits with my father were infrequent, and when I was with him, I wasn't sure that he knew I was there. Even though we were in the same room, there seemed to be a barrier between us that I couldn't penetrate. It was in my father's presence that I first became aware of dark spirits. Even in the sunlight or in a brightly-lit room, there were often shadows hovering close to him. I was never able to see faces or clear images in these dark spots, but I felt them as a sad and confusing heaviness that hung in the air like a shroud. Although I wanted my father's love and at times felt an impulse to run into his arms or sit close to him, I never could. There were forces that seemed to be moving me around like a chess piece and I mostly quietly went along with them.

Chapter 4

Spirits as Family

After my father left, my mother went to work full-time as a waitress at one of those quaint-looking New England restaurants on a winding country road. She worked nights and was usually already gone by the time we got home from school. During the week I often saw her only when saying good-by in the morning. Most Sunday mornings she dropped us at the front door of the Baptist Church. More than once we ran out of gas on the way there. When the car began to sputter my mother would frantically pat the dashboard and say, "Come on, Bessie, you can make it." It never worked, the car eventually came to a stop in the middle of the road. My mother, still in her bathrobe, made my brother walk to the nearest open gas station with an empty red jug. The rest of us sat quietly and uncomfortably in our Sunday outfits and waited.

The frequency with which we ran out of gas was a fitting metaphor for Sunday school. It too seemed empty and dry. As we sat in small folding chairs in the church basement, the teacher moved Biblical figures around on a felt board and told stories. We sang a few songs, then headed for the door and started walking home. Somewhere between church and home my mother picked us up.

For a while an array of different babysitters came through our door, most of them teenage girls from the neighborhood. Then came Francine. She went to the Catholic high school and was our babysitter for several years. During the week she slept in my mother's room and my mother slept on the couch. Francine had blue eyes and long brown hair that she twisted around large soda can curlers at night. She was the most beautiful person I knew. Most of her time was spent on the phone and doing homework.

Before and after dinner we were expected to play outside and come home when the street lights went on.

On the nights when my mother was not waitressing, she got dressed up and went out. When she was home, she slept a lot and when awake she was often distracted or overly focused on straightening things out. In her darker moods, she had outbursts of anger and usually found something wrong with the way I dusted, folded laundry or cooked.

Although my mother was loud, potentially violent and unpredictable, she didn't have the dark shadows around her that my father did and I learned how to maneuver around her. Despite her commanding ways, my mother yielded a surprisingly little amount of power over me.

There was a large expanse of woods across from our house with hills, valleys, a creek and train tracks running through it. At the bottom of a steep hill was Cobin's pond and next to it was an old brick mill that was no longer in use. During the mill's heyday it dumped all of its dyes and waste into the pond and it was still polluted. There was a junkyard full of old cars not too far from this. It too hadn't been used in a long time and was overgrown with vegetation and weeds. I wasn't allowed to go to either of these places, but I regularly did.

The train tracks that ran through the woods were just across the street from our house. We had to walk to school and taking the tracks cut the distance in half. In cold Western Massachusetts winters we did everything we could to get to school as quickly as possible. Not only did we walk through the woods and take every shortcut we could think of, we went through yards and over a footbridge in someone's garden.

On the way out the door to school, the last thing my mother would often say was, "Don't take the tracks to school."

"Okay," we answered. Then we headed straight for the woods.

Somedays she would watch us to make sure we took a left

toward the street, instead of a right into the woods. When she did this we walked up the road, then turned down the next street over to get to the woods and the train tracks.

Coming home from school was even more daring. When the last school bell rang the walkers were supposed to line up at the front of the school. Once there, the janitor, a heavy man who wore a tee shirt when it was warm and a dirty-looking jacket in the cold, blew a loud whistle. This was our signal to cross the street. Once we crossed, we waited for the next whistle to cross the next street. We did this until he crossed us over the busiest street, then we were on our own to walk home. The route he took us on went in the opposite direction of our house and made our walk twice as long. All walkers were supposed to go this way but my sister and I didn't care. We devised a detailed plan on how to sneak out the basement back door without being detected. When my brother started school we made him do this with us. Sometimes the janitor would see us and yell and blow his whistle, but we just keep running.

Once at home the babysitter greeted us with a wave while she talked on the phone or watched television and we went our separate ways. This was when my real life began. Even though my mother forbade it, I couldn't wait to get to the woods. It never occurred to me to abide by this rule as I thought that the woods didn't want her.

In the spring and summer, it was easy to disappear into the thick, green vegetation. There were a few favorite spots that I frequented; one was on the side of a hill with a view of the distant mountains and the other one was a little hollow surrounded by trees and covered with vines that you had to crawl through to get into. This is where I listened. Except for birds and the sounds of kids riding their bikes, or yelling and playing in the distance, it was quiet. Breathing in the warm smell of dirt or the scent of a recent rain or honeysuckle blossoms and blackberry bushes, I relaxed and was more comfortable here than anyplace else. I couldn't understand why there were not others like me hiding in these warm green shelters. As I lay in the sunlight looking up at the sky, everything came to life.

The colors, sounds and sensations were more intense and another world emerged. Tingling energy and warmth moved up and down my arms and legs as I became aware of the presence of my spirit friends. They talked to me in whispers and sometimes I saw them in surprising detail. Their messages were mostly simple and easy to understand and I felt comforted. At times they felt distant, and even though I could feel their presence, I couldn't hear or understand them.

Although I often felt Dawn Marie close, it was in the woods that her presence was the strongest. She talked to me about my family and I felt safe and loved when she was close. When I first felt the presence of a fatherly-like male presence, I thought I had made him up. I wanted a father so much I wasn't sure if I was making him up. Then one afternoon I saw him in a field walking toward me and he didn't look anything like my father or any other man that I knew. He was tall with dark hair and he looked young, too young to be a father. Through whispers and thoughts he helped me to understand my parents better and he encouraged me to trust that there was a reason and purpose behind everything that happened. Sometimes when I went to the woods I felt sad, angry or lonely, but it didn't last for long. Even when it was bone-chillingly cold, if I quietly sat and stared into the sky, I felt his warmth and relaxed into it. This was the feeling I longed for and sought out as often as possible.

There was also a woman spirit who was harder to identify. Sometimes she felt like I imagined a grandmother would feel, kind and soft. At other times, she felt more like a no-nonsense warrior who pushed me to take care of myself and be strong. If I was confused or upset, she whispered reassuring messages in my ear.

There were other spirits who belonged to the trees and plants.

They were smaller and playful. On a sunny hill there was a large patch of pussy willows that the spirits hovered close to. They also liked the big green ferns near the stream that ran through the woods. They were mostly fun to watch and some seemed to notice me, but didn't interact.

Huddled in the trees or walking in the snow, I didn't have to carry the heavy burden of emotions, confusion and loneliness alone. Early on, the spirits whispered in my ear that all love was God's love. The love that moved through my parents for me was from God, and if they couldn't give me this love, God would find another way to get it to me. It was mostly in the woods that this love felt the strongest.

At the time I had no language for what I experienced. It was just pleasurable and I didn't want or need to over examine it.

The Spirits Ask Me to Help

Although my mother was a powerful force in my life, it was the spirits that I sought out and listened to. In school, with my family and sometimes with friends, I felt invisible. I never felt this way with the spirits. They were familiar and I felt seen and known. The spirit realm became my go-to for advice, insights and direction.

However, this is not to say that being with the spirits was without challenges. They often told me things that I didn't necessarily like hearing and asked me to do things that I would rather not do.

For instance when I was in elementary school, the spirits nudged me to make friends with Lisa, a thin girl with long braids. We were in the same class, but we were both quiet and stayed to ourselves. Her father was in the air force, and although there were schools on the large military base some of the kids lived in town and went to my school.

Lisa didn't join in and play with the other kids during recess. She sat and ate alone and read books. All this was fine with me as I was more of a loner myself and painfully shy. However, the spirits kept encouraging me to say hello to her and make friends. One day during recess they whispered in my ear to go talk to her.

"Okay, okay," I said.

I thought that they wanted me to make more friends. My mother was always concerned that I didn't have many. I thought maybe the spirits also thought this was a good idea.

When we went in the cafeteria to eat, I smiled and sat next to her. I didn't say anything and thought that for now the smile was enough. The rest of the week, I did the same thing. I sat next to her at lunch and we looked at each other and said a few uninteresting things. Somehow we became friends. Not best arm-in-arm pals who shared secrets, but we did play together and seemed to have an understanding.

Not long into our budding relationship, Lisa was absent for a few days. Then one afternoon the teacher went around the room, desk to desk, and asked us to sign a card for her. She told us that Lisa's father had lost his life in the Vietnam War.

Lisa came back to school a few days later and I sat next to her at recess. She looked sad and I told her that I was sorry that her dad died.

"He'll still be with you. You'll see," I said.

She didn't say anything and it felt good to be able to be her friend. A few weeks after this, Lisa told me that she was moving to be closer to her grandmother. I was glad that I had listened to the spirits and made friends with her.

Not long after Lisa left, the guides were at it again. There was a boy in my class whose ears stuck out. I mean really stuck out. He was teased unmercifully for this and called a monkey or Dumbo, after the cartoon elephant. Although his life had to be hell, he quietly sat at his desk and acted like he didn't notice. One day after being absent for a couple of days, he came back to school wearing a helmet that covered his ears. He wore this all day and

I figured that it was some kind of treatment to encourage his ears to grow toward his head and not away from it. The helmet became an instant source of jokes and constant put-downs. Some of the kids threw things at him when the teacher wasn't looking, and he still sat there and tried to act normal.

Meanwhile the teasing was breaking my heart. I felt his pain and it weakened me. Quiet and invisible to the other kids, I felt powerless to do anything to help him and I felt every mean word and jab that was meant for him.

Sitting in the woods one afternoon, the spirits whispered to me that he needed a friend. They wanted me to help him. I told them that I wasn't good at making friends and didn't want to try. Still, I knew the spirits were right. The next day when my sister came to pick me up from my class, I pointed him out to her. Sandee was good at making friends and knowing what to do. After I told her how he was being teased she suggested I write him a note. Later that day I wrote small one-line notes on little pieces of paper and then folded them up. They said things like, "Don't listen to the mean kids," and "You're okay." Nothing profound, just little things that I hoped would help him to feel better.

The next day I got to class early and slipped the notes into his desk. I never saw him read one and I don't know if he even found them. However, the spirits seemed pleased with my effort and they never brought him up again.

Chapter 5

The Intruder

When I was in the sixth grade my mother met Bob. She had dated other men, but Bob was different. The first time he entered our house he took control and things began to change. Like a seasoned corporate enforcer called in to bring order, he had every intention of shaking up and reorganizing our lives. I wanted Bob to like me.

Visits from my father had dwindled and we rarely saw or heard from him. When we did it was awkward and rushed. He usually took us to the Big Boy restaurant and let us order whatever we wanted. We never went out to eat with my mother, so when we pulled up to the big ceramic statue of Big Boy in his red checkered pants holding a hamburger, we were ecstatic. The restaurant was always busy and loud, and the smell and sound of meat sizzling on the grill was almost overwhelming. My father never ate with us, preferring instead to smoke a cigarette and have a few drinks.

Equating his love with the fried shrimp and strawberry and whipped cream waffles, we ate like ravenous stray dogs who could never get enough. While he looked out the window or at other customers, we downed our food with barely a word exchanged between us. Then he took us home. After a stiff kiss, we made our way into the house, already looking forward to his next visit. However, he was unpredictable. More than once we sat on our front step waiting for him until it got dark and we went to bed.

Like an outgoing tide, my parents' attention easily drifted away. Both of them were preoccupied with more important things, like bowling and drinking. Not Bob, he was attentive, examined our every move and critiqued it. He filled our lives with activity and kept us on a short leash. We went camping, roller skating and climbed mountains, all under his watchful eye. Bob prided himself on taking on challenges, and closed roads due to snow and ice didn't deter him. He would load us into the old station wagon and heroically make it to the base of the mountain where we waded, sometimes in waist-deep snow, up an impassable trail. Despite our objections he corralled me and my three siblings into participating in whatever he deemed important.

My siblings and my mother all seemed to love and trust Bob. Even though I wanted to and tried to feel the same way, there was something about him that repelled me. Although he was enthusiastic in a take charge kind of way, I didn't feel that he was being genuine. My intuitive sense about him didn't match the outer picture and I was confused.

Although Bob acted like a happy camp counselor, something about him made me uncomfortable and apprehensive. In my attempt to have him like me I tried to be more friendly and outgoing, but it wasn't easy. It was obvious to me that he was putting on a show. Although he acted positive and enthusiastic about being a father, I could feel his anger and frustration. There was no affection or emotional warmth coming from him and I was perplexed that no one seemed to be aware of this. I tried to push through my reservations, but I couldn't. There was a darkness, like a scent coming from him, that repelled me.

One Sunday evening after a long day of hiking my mother and Bob were in the kitchen making dinner. I went to get a glass of water and found them laying on the linoleum kitchen floor in front of the stove wrapped in each other's arms and kissing. Next to them, black smoke poured out of the stove as our toasted cheese and bacon sandwiches burnt to a crisp. As smoke filled the house, I stood staring down at them wrapped in an embrace, completely unaware to what was happening around them. My mother seemed to be under his spell and oblivious to anything happening outside of their romance. I felt only dread and concern about his overwhelming influence.

Exiled to the Cousins

Within a few months of meeting, my mother and Bob got married. During the reception held in our backyard, my sister told me that they had to get married. She then led me into my mother's room and showed me a book about pregnancy on her night stand and maternity clothes hanging in her closet.

Several months later on a warm summer day, my mother big and pregnant decided to take us all to the local pool to cool down. As I went to get in the car a flash of dread and anxiety came over me. Even though I wanted to go, I couldn't get in the car and told my mother that I had a stomachache. She shrugged her shoulders, shut the door and they all took off. Alone in the house my anxiety increased. When it started to get dark and they still had not come home my fears were confirmed, something was wrong. Later that evening, my siblings and Bob finally walked in the door and told me they had been in an accident. My mother was still in the hospital.

The next morning, Bob's sister who I had met just once pulled into the driveway. My brother and I were told to pack our things as we were going to go stay with her family. They lived in a small house in another state, and as kind as they were to welcome us in, it was uncomfortable. There were holes in the walls, and when one of my cousins saw me look at a big gash in his door, he laughed and told me that he put his foot through it. No stranger to violent behavior, I knew to keep my mouth shut and not get into trouble.

For three long weeks, I followed my newly-appointed girl cousin around the neighborhood as she lit fires in the woods and stalked a neighborhood girl threatening to beat her up. My brother's situation was even more difficult. He had to contend with two boy cousins who were both older and considerably outweighed him. Like my girl cousin, they caused their own mischief and mayhem. Everyone in this family liked to fight and much of the day was spent listening to them make fun of and insult their neighbors. In the evening we all sat in the living room watching television and eating donuts or cake while they argued and came close to blows. My brother and I would pass each other in the woods or on the street, each with our respective cousins, and shoot each other a look of desperation. Most nights I lay awake feeling overwhelmed by the thick anger and chaos that I felt in this house.

The day before school was to begin, we were taken home. It was just turning dark when we arrived and we were immediately ushered into my mother's bedroom. Curled up in her bed in the darkened room she looked small and weak and told us that she lost the baby, a boy. Then she turned over on her side and silently faced the wall.

The next day after school, I headed for the woods. In one of my favorite spots nestled against a tree, I waited for the spirits to come close. As the sun was setting, I felt the familiar warmth of my sister, Dawn Marie, and asked her if my brother was with her. Not receiving a reply, I waited and looked for him, but I couldn't feel or sense him and couldn't understand why. I tried the next day and many times after and never felt his presence.

A few months later the spirits told me that the soul that would have been my brother found another family and he was no longer in the spirit realm.

"There was another birth opportunity that his soul took advantage of and he became someone else's brother and son," Dawn Marie said.

"Why didn't you do that?" I asked.

"It wasn't part of my plan to be born in a physical body. I knew this from the beginning. I love you and your family," she whispered into my ear. "I wanted to be a guiding presence and help all of you. The pregnancy allowed me to be closer."

Chapter 6

Angel Dog and Demon Dad

After returning from exile at my cousins, everything changed. Bob was now in charge and took over discipline which he deemed necessary and serious business. By this time, I had several years of independence under my belt. Raised by distracted babysitters who encouraged us to come and go and handle our own stuff, I learned how to carefully work around my mother's authority and felt no desire to be told what to do.

This was not Bob's idea of parenting. He believed in authority and swift punishment for not following rules and expectations. Newly married and mourning the loss of another child, my mother offered no resistance to the new regime and became his complicit sidekick. Not that she needed his encouragement. Prone to outbursts of anger, anything within her reach was a potential weapon. She could twist a hairbrush around like a confident gunslinger and either whack me on the head or send it flying across the room and hit me straight on. Once Bob took over the discipline, the anger and violence voltage was pumped up. My mother and Bob seemed to feed off one another's moods and meanness. It felt as if being abusive was a hobby and bonding experience for them.

There was a prescribed way to do everything from fold a towel to line up the silverware on the table. A small indiscretion could lead to a swift blow and sharp ridicule. The mood became critical, sullen and sad. While to the outside world we were lucky to have a father like Bob, there was a cruelty of power that was only expressed behind closed doors.

It became more difficult to find the time to be alone in the woods. Fortunately, this didn't deter the spirits. When lying in my bed, alone in the basement and sometimes in the company of others, I was able to feel their presence and hear their whispers. Like a plant in the dry desert in need of water, I relied on them.

With the help of the spirits, I did my best to adapt and walk the line. However, when Holly came into my life, my allegiance to the new order ended. A shepherd mix, Holly was just six weeks old when we got her. From the moment I saw her I believed that she was an angel. There was just something about her that felt good and holy. Confined to a wooden pen in the dark, cold basement, I played with her before and after school and as much as I could in the evening. Alone most of the day and night, her cries of loneliness tore me apart. When she got a little bigger, Bob tied her up in the backyard, and when she cried and barked, he went out and beat her. When winter came I sat by the window and watched Holly shiver in the cold. During a particularly bad snowstorm, my sister went outside with some old boards and tried to build her a shelter. It was pathetic and didn't stand up for long. As I listened to her sad whine, something in me wilted and died. Powerless to do anything to help her, my heart filled with anger and hatred for Bob. One day I came home from school and Holly was gone. My mother said that she took her to a farmer and I never found out what really happened.

Bob's consistent cold and callous behavior extended beyond Holly and no one was spared. In Bob and my mother's sideshow of cruel theatrics, my siblings and I each played a role and had no choice in the part we were assigned. Dinner was the most dangerous time of the day. Before we ate, my mother read a passage from the *Methodist Daily Prayers and Reflections* book. Once we said amen, the carnage began. It always started under the simple guise of sharing what each of us did during the day, but it didn't take long before someone was singled out for interrogation. Whatever was said was picked apart and used to taunt or ridicule. My sister was the most vocal and Bob would bait her into a discussion which quickly dissolved into put-downs and teasing her. My special niche was being a selfish, rotten brat and I was continually reminded of this. There was probably some truth to the rotten brat part. I was rebellious and didn't care if I was punished. Sometimes I walked right into the trap and said and did what I knew would bring their fury down on me.

With a straightforward look of authority Bob did his best to intimidate. "If you say that one more time, I am going to take my belt off," he often said.

I took this as a dare, and whatever it was, I said it. Then sure enough the belt came off. My mother leaped from her seat and held me down while Bob hit me, over and over. I almost always fought it. I squirmed and screamed like crazy. I wanted them to know that they couldn't silence me. Of course no one cared, but I didn't want to give up and I didn't want to submit without a fight.

At times my stubbornness served me well. When I was older, it was my obstinate nature that made it possible for me to work with skeptical detectives and provide psychic information about serious crimes. In one particular murder investigation one of the two detectives I was working with believed that psychics were a complete sham and let me know it. He underestimated my stubbornness. I wouldn't give up and eventually identified the killer.

However, when young, I wasn't always able to discern a good time to be stubborn from just walking into a lot of trouble. It was also easier for me to become a target, than to see and feel my siblings get picked on and beaten. There was something I could go to. My spirit friends and an invisible sustaining force were always there for me, so I ran interference. Something in me wouldn't give in and comply with the tyranny. I didn't want to lose myself, this was all I had.

Consequently, I got hit for such things as: having a look on my face, making sounds and not answering a question the right way. It was a minefield and anything could trigger a beating.

When they became intense, I inwardly repeated to myself that no one and nothing could touch or harm me. Focusing inward, I escaped to a place above my physical body and became skilled at detaching from what was happening. Although I was aware of and acutely sensitive to feelings of anger and physical pain, I imagined that a shield surrounded and protected me.

From this inner detached vantage point, I saw my mother's eyes glaze over with rage and become almost hypnotic. Her intensity seemed to have little to do with what I said or did, and in the midst of her rage she often said, "You're a bad seed. I'll kill you before you reach the age of sixteen."

I believed her and continued to fight.

Bob, too, seemed to be fighting a battle that had nothing to do with me. His eyes became red and the sweat that poured from him had an odd unsettling scent that progressively became stronger and more repulsive. He was foreign to me. An invader who saw me as easy prey. I was angry at my mother for letting him in and wanted to show them they could not touch me. While they yelled and hit or pushed me against the wall, I knew that my body was not me. I found it curious that they thought that they were affecting me, because I knew that I was someplace else.

However, despite my ability to withdraw and pull my energy in, the effects were still devastating and profound. I felt odd and different and the constant put-downs and physical rage increased my despair and lowered my self-esteem. In lonely moments, I believed there was something truly and innately wrong with me.

As the abuse continued it became more difficult to connect with the spirits the way that I had when I was younger. The warm feelings of comfort and the soft face of my spirit friends seemed out of my reach. I started smoking cigarettes, took long walks and didn't care if I got in trouble. As often as possible I went to one of my favorite spots in the woods where I sat in the sun and listened.

My only question to the spirits was, "Why?" I asked it over and over. Sometimes I felt the familiar warmth of their presence move through me and I intuitively knew that everything would be all right. Yet this was little comfort. I still had to go home.

Chapter 7

Ghosts in the Church Basement

We went to a Congregationalist church which my mother took to with a lusty devotion. She got involved in or spearheaded many activities and we were expected to spend as much time at church as she did. We went to Sunday school, youth groups, revivals, hayrides, spaghetti dinners and when the church had a yoga class we went to that too. However, my sister and I never took to church. Instead we often used it as a way to protest my mother's control.

As teenagers my sister and I were not allowed to use makeup or wear pants or nylon stockings. This was the seventies and even though the school allowed girls to wear pants, we were confined to the dark ages of knee socks, dresses and skirts. No bell-bottoms, paisley flowing peasant shirts or dangling earrings for us. Appearances were important for my mother.

On Sunday mornings my mother went to church early for choir practice, we followed later with Bob. Seated behind the minister's pulpit, a look of horror would spread across my mother's face when my sister and I walked into the sanctuary wearing our favorite church outfits. Mine included florescent orange fishnet stockings and a bright green skirt that I pulled up and folded into a miniskirt. As I watched my mother scowl at me, I sat in the cold pew and listened to sermons that never made much sense to me.

As often as I could I slipped out of the church pew and went to the basement to smoke cigarettes. One cold winter's day under the guise of helping out in the nursery, I snuck down the stairs to the dark musty basement. Surrounded by hymnals and folding chairs, I knew I was not alone. In a dark corner I felt the presence of an unfamiliar spirit who seemed as confused as I was. For a moment fear gripped me and I wanted to flee and head for the stairs. Instead I stopped and felt it reach out to me. This spirit was unlike the ones that I was familiar with; it was not warm and loving. Instead it felt scared and lonely and I knew that, like me, it too felt lost. Although I didn't know what to do to help it, I sent it the message that I understood.

After this I began to feel these wispy and hollow figures other places as well. At Bob's parents' house, I encountered an older man, who sat in the corner of the kitchen. He was quiet and didn't seem to notice me and we never interacted. Going in my friend's home after school one day, I saw the clear image of a man staring back at me from a hallway mirror. After telling my friend about him, her mother made her break off her friendship with me. These encounters didn't scare or disturb me, and most of the time these spirits never interacted with me. They mostly seemed confused and lost, and I wanted to help them. Years later when I developed a deeper understanding of the spirit realm, I realized that they were ghosts or lost souls.

It was not only ghosts that I encountered. My awareness of other spirits was also intensifying. Unable to spend much time outdoors in the winter, I spent more time at home in the basement. Although it was unfinished, it had an old couch and a small gas heater. One afternoon as I got up from the couch I became overwhelmed with dizziness. I was so drowsy I couldn't keep my eyes open. I laid down, closed my eyes and suddenly saw a golden white cloud-like image and in the center of it was an old man with kind eyes. He smiled and I felt peaceful and relaxed. Even though I didn't know who this was, he felt familiar and I knew he loved me. There was no fear or apprehension.

Unlike the ghosts, this spirit saw me and I knew that he wanted me to know that he was with me. It felt as if he was sending me a message, but I couldn't stay focused and take in everything that was happening. A soft humming and relaxing vibration moved through me and I wanted to let whatever was happening continue for as long as possible. Then as quickly as it began, it was over. No longer dizzy or tired, I felt rejuvenated and a bit confused.

During Bob's dark reign, I took any opportunity that got me away from home. When a friend invited me to join her and her mother on a camping trip at the beach, I readily accepted.

We camped in a pine forest in a large tent, not too far from the beach. Early one morning while lying in my sleeping bag listening to birds chirping, I closed my eyes and saw an image of a man with dark hair. He was not aware of me and appeared to be lost and looking for someone. A moment later, a woman appeared next to him who I knew was his mother. They hugged and seemed happy to be together. Then the image was gone.

Later that morning while eating a stale muffin, I asked my friend's mother if she was an Elvis Presley fan. Her eyes lit up and she enthusiastically described in detail a concert of his she attended years earlier. Later that afternoon on our way to the grocery store, we heard on the radio that Elvis Presley had died. A shiver went down my spine and I realized that the vision of the man that I saw earlier that morning looked like Elvis Presley. Never having had much interest in his music, I couldn't understand why I saw him and his mother.

A few months later while lying in bed one morning, I heard a man singing, "You can lean on me." Half-awake, I closed my eyes and listened. Suddenly a bright light that I thought might be the sun appeared. In the light was the man, still singing, "You can lean on me." I realized that this was Jesus. His voice was loud and I didn't know what to do or why he was there.

Slowly he faded away, leaving me with more questions. Why was I having visions of both Elvis and Jesus? Although unexplainable experiences were becoming the norm, I tried not to give them too much thought.

Chapter 8

The Spirits Whisper of Freedom

By the time I was a junior in high school, conditions at home had further deteriorated. The arguing and fighting between my mother and Bob reached a fevered pitch and there was constant tension and drama. During dinner one evening, my mother cheerfully announced that Bob was going to adopt me and my sister. A couple of years earlier, he had legally adopted my two brothers and now it was our turn.

I steadfastly refused and my mother threatened to send me to a place called Bright Side, a psychiatric home for troubled children. However, there was a cost to my resistance. My mother and Bob's anger and rage intensified and every day became a battle. Reluctantly, I eventually agreed. I was worn down and all I wanted to do was graduate from high school and leave home. My psychic awareness was increasing and I clung to it as evidence that there was something more powerful than what I was experiencing. Sensations, awareness and feelings of otherworldly love and guidance sustained me and gave me hope for the future. The spirit world was sane and safe.

Before I was officially adopted I had to tell my father. Although I had not seen or talked to him for years, I still loved him and considered him my father. Christmas gifts, birthday cards and visits had long since stopped and I couldn't remember the last time we spoke. When I called him and asked him to meet with me and my sister, he must have known it was important because he arrived on time.

While we drove to an ice cream shop, he talked about the impressive features of his new car. Once in the restaurant I sat in a brightly-colored booth facing him. I couldn't look him in the eye and twisted my paper napkin around my finger until it turned red then blue. The pain felt good and I wondered if maybe this might kill me or at least cause me to faint and get out of this situation. As I watched my ice cream melt, I regretted ever having agreed to be adopted.

My father, the salesman, had a way of charming others. Despite not hearing from him for years, he comfortably sat across from us, joked and made small talk. It was like no time had passed and he was the same Dad.

Finally I said, "Bob wants to adopt us."

He didn't seem surprised or shocked and said, "You're my girls and I don't want to lose you."

"We don't have a choice," I said.

After a long pause, he said, "Why are you doing this to me?"

My heart lurched and beat loud in my chest. Yet all I could say was, "Don't make this harder on us. You don't know what it's like."

My father looked sad as we got back in the car and silently drove home.

Adrift with no emotional anchor, my feelings of alienation with my family reached a new low and extended into the spirit realm. My heart was closed and I felt let down by the spirits. It had been my hope that they would help to make my life easier and better. Yet, things just seemed to get worse. I wanted their love and I listened for their whispers, but I had a growing resistance to connecting with them. I flip-flopped back and forth from seeking them out and being angry with them.

A few weeks after meeting with my father, my sister and I went before a judge. Wearing a new dress and sitting uncomfortably in a cold marble-floored waiting area, I decided to answer all of the judge's questions honestly. My last chance of getting out of this was my hope that he would ask me if Bob hit me or if I loved him and wanted him to be my father.

My sister went first, and when she came out of his office without looking at me, I knew I was doomed.

Sitting behind his cluttered desk, the judged stared down at a paper he was holding and said, "What kind of chores do you do at home?"

I went through my long list and anxiously waited for the next question. But, that was it.

"Thank you," he said. "You can go back to the waiting room."

We were Bob's official daughters. When I went back to school the next day, I had the embarrassing task of having to tell my teachers that my last name had changed. Two of them asked me to stay after class to ask me if I had gotten married.

Being officially adopted didn't make life at home easier. Instead, conditions got worse. It was my senior year in high school and I was counting the days to graduation. Still it was hard to ignore that Bob and my mother's relationship was falling apart. For days at a time, Bob refused to talk to anyone. He would come home from work, eat dinner, watch television and act like none of us existed. If you asked him a question he would ignore it and look the other way. He started writing notes in red lipstick on the mirrors. He wrote things like, *Eat Without Me*, or *I am not going to give you any money*.

My mother's moods became even more unstable and I never knew what to expect. She would cry uncontrollably and yell and hit Bob. He was a big man and just stared straight ahead and acted like she wasn't there.

Less than a year after the adoption, Bob wrote a note on the mirror in his bedroom. It said, *Goodby*. Then he packed his things and left.

I was happy to see him go and hoped that my mother felt the same way. Unfortunately she wanted him back and talked about him incessantly. A few months after Bob left, I too packed my bags and loaded an old car that I had saved from the junkyard. On my way out the door to go to college, my mother fell to the floor and started weeping and shaking. Wrapping herself around my legs, she pleaded with me to stay.

"Don't go, I need you here to help me," she both demanded and weakly requested.

Her mood suddenly changed to anger, and she then began to accuse me of being selfish and not caring what happened to her.

Numb and not knowing what to do, I stood silent and frozen.

A soft repetitive whisper startled me. "Go, it's okay, go," I heard over and over. The warm feeling of a hand on my back pointed me toward the door.

My mother's grip around my legs loosened and I picked up my things and left.

Part II Saved by the Spirits

Chapter 9

A Visit with a Priest

I chose the college I attended for two reasons. I could afford the tuition and it was located in the foothills of the Berkshire Mountains. A small state school that had no dorms, it lacked the more interesting academic and social opportunities of bigger schools. However, when I saw the boulder-laden river that wound down the mountain and through the small campus, I was hooked.

The freedom that I longed for had finally arrived and it was exhilarating. In this new life, I wanted to be what I considered normal and like everyone else. I was ready to put the past behind me and that included being psychic. While I had previously clung to the whispers of guidance and the feelings of comfort from the spirit world, I was ready to let it all go. Although my connection to the unseen had sustained and nurtured me, I thought it time to go it on my own.

Money was tight and I was paying for school and living expenses from what I had saved as a lifeguard at the city pool, babysitter and check-out girl at a small store. The area was going through an economic downturn and money was tight. Eventually I found a job cleaning offices at the school and as a dishwasher at night in a restaurant.

However, as much as I needed to focus on school and work, my psychic switch was turned up and not off as I had hoped. The more I tried not to be psychic and see spirits, the more powerfully it seemed to surface. During the day I did my best to suppress psychic interruptions. However, at night I was flooded with psychic dreams. Most of which seemed to be a preview of was going to happen the following day or week.

For the most part there was nothing profound or enlightening about what I psychically tuned into. For instance, one night I dreamt I saw an opal ring with an unusual cut stone on display in a jewelry store. The next day on my way to catch the bus to school, I passed a jewelry store window and saw the exact ring that I had seen the night before. While sitting in class one day, I saw an image of a friend of mine trying to talk me into getting my hair cut. She had never mentioned this to me previously, but the next day this same friend gave me the name of her hairdresser and suggested I give her a call. In quick images, feelings and awareness, I saw and knew such things as what the essay questions on an exam would be. When and how my work hours were going to change, that the head of the college was going to resign and that the Catholic pope was going to die. Despite my desire to experience a psychic- and spirit-free new beginning, I was glad when I still felt my spirit friends close and heard their whispers.

Confused and overwhelmed by the increase and intensity of recent psychic experiences, I didn't want to keep this part of me secret any longer. I longed to finally confide in someone. When my friend Colleen came for a visit I patiently listened while she talked about the cute boys at her school. When she finished, I took a deep breath and nervously described just a bit about the psychic encounters that I was experiencing. It was clear by the blank look on her face that this was not what she was expecting me to say.

After a few moments of uncomfortable silence, she said, "I think you should go talk to a priest."

"Why a priest?" I asked.

"My priest has helped me so much and they know a lot about these supernatural kind of things."

I wasn't convinced that seeing a priest was the answer to understanding my psychic experiences, but she was so passionate and sure that this would help, I agreed.

Not long after on a windy and chilly day I anxiously stood in front of the Catholic church just down the street from me. The massive old brick rectory loomed over me like a dark cloud. I didn't have a good feeling about going in and wished that I had kept my mouth shut about being psychic. Before I could back out, Colleen took me by the arm and together we climbed the tall steps and opened the large wooden door. It was dark inside, and as we stood there not knowing where to go and what to do, a nun dressed in a grey habit greeted us. My friend told her that I wanted to talk to the priest.

"I see, can I ask why?" she said.

"She is having some unusual experiences and needs guidance," Colleen looked desperate when she said this.

"Please follow me," the nun replied.

She led me down a red-carpeted hall and into a large dark-paneled room full of bookcases and religious pictures and other Catholic-looking things. I went in alone and the nun told me to have a seat. After she left the room, I started to sweat and felt a little panicky. As was my custom, I turned my fear into anger and started to get mad at myself for even asking for help. Several minutes later, an older man with a head that looked too small for his body came in. He was dressed in a black robe and wore tiny glasses. I assumed he was the priest. After taking a seat behind a massive wooden desk that looked as if it might swallow him, he asked me what I wanted to talk about.

I can't remember exactly what I told him, but I blurted out something about dreams that told the future and being psychic.

Once I finished, he quickly looked up from his desk. "Have you ever been to a psychiatrist?" he asked.

"No," I said and headed for the door. "Thank you for your time."

Not knowing if he was going to summon a church psychiatrist or the police who would take me to some kind of facility, I brushed past my friend and left the church as fast as I could.

Embarrassed and ashamed of what the priest had said to

me, I thought that maybe there was something truly different and wrong with me. Although I didn't think that I was crazy, I wasn't so sure that others might not see me this way. When pushed for details from my friend, I simply told her that he was not much help and decided to keep my experiences to myself from now on.

Chapter 10

Hitchhiking On the Psychic Highway

One late afternoon on my way to my job cleaning offices at the college, I stopped to watch the cars from a highway overpass disappear into the mountains. I felt a tug in my heart and knew that I would soon be on that road, a dot on the horizon vanishing into the distant hills. I didn't know why or where I would be going, but I intuitively knew change was coming.

When finished with the offices, I jumped in my car to be on time for my dishwashing job at a restaurant in the next town. As I crossed the road out of the school parking lot, the car stalled and died. After many attempts to revive her, I realized she wasn't coming back to life. This wasn't too surprising; I had saved the old Ford from the junkyard a year earlier. It was in such bad shape that when it rained or snowed, water shot up through the holes in the rusted floorboards soaking the inside of the car.

The loss of my car sent me into a tailspin. Washing dishes paid the rent on my attic apartment and my tuition, but I needed a car to get there. I still had the office cleaning job but it was only a few hours a week and didn't pay much. Every day I unsuccessfully searched for a job. If it was the spring or summer I would have been able to work on a farm, but the weather was getting colder and many places were closing for the winter.

A few weeks after my car died, my mother called and asked if she could pick me up and take me home for the weekend. Surprised by this unexpected offer, I agreed. A few days later on a rainy evening, she pulled up in front of my apartment and honked the horn. As soon as I got in the car, I knew that I was in trouble. My mother's face looked tense and her hands gripped the steering wheel.

Before we made it to the highway and without turning her

head to look at me, she said, "I'm not here to take you home. I talked to Reverend Williams and he believes you need tough love. You need to straighten out. I've tried with you and have had no success. You're on your own now."

I was stunned and wondered what she was talking about. I was already on my own and I wasn't sure what I was straightening out from. While in high school, I occasionally drank and smoked pot with my friends. However, once I left home I was too busy and overwhelmed with school, work and with the psychic phenomena that I was experiencing. I had no desire to further alter my consciousness. When I asked her if she thought I was on drugs or drinking, she told me that she was not going to play games with me. She then pulled over at a gas station and told me to get out. It was dark and I walked home in the cold rain. Although I was no stranger to loneliness and despair, my self-esteem was at an all-time low. I knew my mother well enough to know that there was nothing that would change her mind.

Although I had no plans to return home, my mother's declaration of tough love came at a lousy time. My rent payment was coming due and I had no money. When I shared my financial difficulties with my friend Colleen she told me that she was in a similar situation.

"My dad told me he can't pay for my dorm room," she said. "He wants me to leave school and move home, maybe go to a community college. That's the last thing I want to do. I've been thinking, there's plenty of work in Florida. It's getting cold here. Lots of students go down there for the winter to work and save money. With the tourist season, it'll be easy to get jobs."

"I guess it beats being kicked out of my apartment and homeless," I said.

Less than a week later we packed our backpacks with summer clothes and headed to Florida. We decided to take the train to Washington DC, about a 10-hour trip, then hitchhike the rest of the way. Not a brilliant plan, but we had so little money this is what we went with.

In DC we stepped off of the train into the cold dark night and headed to a maze of highways not far from the station. After finding a southbound road sign, we stood under a light post and stuck out our nervous thumbs into the heavy and loud traffic.

Although I had hitchhiked many times, this was nothing like the gentle rolling hills of New England. As I stood in the dark and looked out over the mass of headlights coming toward me, I instinctively sought out my spirit guides and pleaded with them for help. Although I had vowed to try and go it alone, I hoped they were still with me. Inwardly I pleaded with them to send someone safe our way. The first car that stopped looked fairly beat up. A young guy about our age opened the door and asked where we were going.

"We're headed to Florida," I said.

There was another guy in the car and they both started laughing.

"You're going the wrong way. Come on in, we'll take you to the right highway."

About fifteen minutes later they let us out on a highway ramp and pointed down the road, "You wanna go that way."

Back out in the cold night, I once again turned to my guides for help.

"Send the cars love," they whispered in my ear. "You'll attract positive energy this way."

Sending love to the cars seemed a little silly, but I went ahead and tried. Soon a small blue car pulled over and came to a stop. A young blond-haired man opened the door and invited us in.

"I'm on my way back to college and have to be in class early in the morning. Would you mind if we take turns driving?" he asked. "I've been behind the wheel all day and I'm exhausted."

"Sure, I can take over," I volunteered.

Within an hour, he asked me to drive and he crawled into the back seat and fell asleep. When we got to the town where he lived, I woke him.

"Why don't you spend the night on my couch," he said.

The next morning he offered us Pop-Tarts and dropped us off at a highway entrance ramp.

It felt good to be out of the city. The roads had less traffic and it was warmer. Bolstered by our good luck the night before and halfway to Florida we felt more confident. We stuck out our thumbs and again I asked my spirit friends for help. Focusing on the cars that came our way, I was surprised when a large tractor trailer pulled over. I had never ridden in such a big vehicle, but we ran to it and climbed up the passenger side. A middle-aged man wearing a baseball cap and a tee shirt that just covered his protruding belly opened the door. With a thick Southern accent he said, "Y'all get on up here," and patted the empty seat next to him.

My traveling partner Colleen was the last person that you would expect to be hitchhiking and climbing into the cab of a tractor trailer. She was as sweet and gentle as she looked. Always seeing the positive in others, she expected the best in every situation and never stopped smiling. I was more skeptical, and while she sweetly smiled and thanked the driver, I looked around the cab and wondered what we were getting into.

Colleen sat closest to the trucker on the edge of a bed compartment where I assumed he slept. There was constant noise and static coming from his CB radio that had a cup of tobacco chew spit leaning against it. Other truckers were breaking in and reporting road conditions, police sightings and using trucker language that I didn't fully understand. The trucker did his best to make small talk and lectured us about life on the road. He told us he was going all the way to Miami, and because we had no firm destination we decided to go there too.

Later that afternoon we pulled into a truck stop and sat at a booth under a buzzing overhead fluorescent light. A few minutes later another trucker and his girlfriend joined us. After some small talk it became obvious that the meeting had been set up to encourage one of us to drive with the new trucker who was also going to Miami. Our trucker said that there was not enough room for both of us in his truck. I was against the idea, but the truckers insisted and Colleen said that she would stay with our trucker. Reluctantly, I agreed to ride in the new truck. Something felt off, but I brushed off my creepy intuitive gut feeling.

Once in the truck I sat in the passenger seat and the girlfriend sat in the middle and flirted with the driver. A short time later we pulled into another stop. The driver parked away from the other trucks in a mostly empty lot. With my psychic radar going a bit crazy, I realized I was being set up and had to find a way out. Unfortunately the truck had an automatic door lock that I couldn't open.

When the trucker turned off the engine, the girlfriend announced that she was going to give me some alone time with the trucker. The last thing I wanted was to be alone with him. I told them I had to use the restroom and they exchanged glances. The girlfriend then quickly maneuvered herself between me and the door while the trucker put his arm around me. The door opened and the girlfriend jumped out. As she did this one of my guides sent me a message to jam the door. Instinctively and without thought, I pushed the strap of my backpack with my foot to the bottom of door so that it wouldn't close. Sliding out from the trucker's hug, I grabbed my backpack and jumped out of the cab.

Without turning back I went in search of Colleen. I didn't know if they had pulled into the stop but I had to check. It was getting dark as I frantically ran up and down the rows of parked trucks. Eventually I saw a red-hooded truck, climbed up the steps of the passenger door and saw the trucker's familiar tobacco spit cup and sunglasses. The door was locked and the seats empty, but the curtain to the sleeping compartment was closed. I banged on the window and called her name. I kept this up until the curtain opened and she slid out to the passenger seat. She had tears in her eyes and a glazed-over fearful look.

"Get out," I yelled to her.

She opened the door and I pulled her out. As we quickly walked toward the restaurant, I asked her what happened.

Once in a brightly-lit booth she said, "I dozed off on the bed while we were driving and woke up with him on top of me. I started to cry and shake and couldn't stop. He asked me what was wrong and I just kept crying. He finally got off of me and then we heard you banging on the door."

"We need to find another ride," I said. I was more angry then scared and wanted to find the truckers and yell at them. However, Colleen was more forgiving.

"If we don't split up I think we can still ride with my trucker," she said.

"Are you kidding," I said. "No way, who knows what he'll do next."

"The worst is over. I think he will be all right. He did get off of me and didn't push it," she said.

I wasn't convinced. As we sat there wondering what to do and too numb to eat, her trucker came in and sat beside Colleen. He said something stupid to be funny and she laughed. They both acted like everything was normal.

"Can we both ride with you?" she asked. "We don't want to split up and no funny business."

"I guess I can take you two young beavers down to Miami," he said. "You'll have to hide in the sleep compartment when we pull into the weigh stations."

Colleen smiled and continued to charm him. The rest of the trip was uneventful. Back in the truck Colleen and I shared the passenger seat and nodded off from time to time. For the next twenty-four hours we only stopped for the driver to sleep a few hours and to eat. Every so often, he got on his CB radio and boasted that he had "two beavers on a bun" which is trucker talk for females in the cab. I remained suspicious and untrusting, and Colleen laughed and carried on with him like they were best friends.

Chapter 11

Watched Over

We stepped out of the truck and into the bright sunshine of Florida. Grateful that we had safely made it to Miami, we thanked the trucker and got out of the cab in high spirits. The air had a heavy, spicy smell, and the heat and humidity was stifling. We quickly shed our winter coats, boots and sweaters. With no car and no map we wandered around for several hours wondering what to do. Late in the afternoon we spotted a run-down apartment complex with a "For Rent" sign. Even though the small one-bedroom apartment was shabby, it had a bed and a few other pieces of furniture so we rented it for the week.

The next afternoon after filling out applications at restaurants, hotels and stores, we made our way back to the apartment. When we got there, several boys who looked to be about our age were lounging around the front door. They immediately started asking us questions.

"What you here for? Where your house at? Why you staying here?"

We tried to answer their questions, but this didn't satisfy their curiosity. It eventually became clear that we were the only white girls and the only white people living in the area and they couldn't quite believe it. Without being invited they came into our apartment, sat on our couch and acted like they had every right to be there.

One of the guys who acted like the leader told us that he and his crew were willing to watch out for us. What he meant by this was that they were not going to leave. Now and then one or two went on an errand or left for a short time, but there were always a couple of guys sleeping on the couch or sitting on the front stoop. Apparently we needed to be watched over and protected from less trustworthy members of the community. Despite guarding us around the clock, they never made any sexual or other demands or used drugs.

For the next few days we continued to search the want ads and fill out job applications with no luck. Eventually we came across an ad for waitress positions at a yacht club on one of the Florida Keys. Without hesitation we walked to the long stretch of highway and stuck out our thumbs. Within a few minutes a man in a small convertible pulled over, and an hour later, he dropped us off at the front gate of the resort. The large club was like a small town with restaurants, stores, beaches, condos, large homes and a marina.

We were hired that day and offered free room and board. The staff housing consisted of four long rows of cinderblock buildings. Each unit had one room with a small window and shared a bathroom with the adjoining unit. The dining hall was a bigger cinderblock room where leftover food from the restaurants was served twice a day.

After collecting our things and saying good-by to our bodyguard friends, we moved into the cinderblock building. Just as it was getting dark, there was a knock on our door. Colleen jumped to open it and wrapped her arms around her brother. Without looking at me, she began to throw her things into her backpack. The same one she had unpacked a few hours ago.

"What's going on?" I asked.

"I thought you knew I was coming to pick Colleen up," her brother said. "You can ride back with us."

"I have no place to go back to and no money. At least here I have a job and someplace to live," I said.

The next morning I got up before dawn, put on my bright yellow uniform that looked much more friendly than I felt, and made my way to the dining room for my first day of work.

By the Pool

Even though there were people of all nationalities and backgrounds, and young and old in the employee housing, I felt more alone and vulnerable after Colleen left. At night people gathered around the pool where there was a lot of liquor, drugs, loud music and occasional fights. I had to be at work before dawn. So I did my best to tune out the noise and keep drunk males from getting in my room. Although I barricaded my door, this didn't stop them from pounding and trying to push their way in while I lay sleepless and tense curled up on my wiry small bed.

One afternoon while sitting in the shade and reading close to the pool, I saw Kari, a young woman about my age who I worked with. From the start she seemed to dislike me, but I didn't take it too personally as she didn't seem to like the other waitresses either. As I watched her, I saw that a cocoon-like shroud of red and grey energy surrounded her. It felt heavy, angry and sad. Unexpectedly I felt my heart open and a wave of soft and compassionate energy drifted from me toward her. It felt as if a little angel was watching out for her. The warm feelings moving through my heart were confusing and I felt moved to reach out and try to befriend her.

For the next couple of days we worked different shifts and I thought of clever ways to approach her when I next saw her. However, one morning I learned that she was fired after getting into an argument with the manager. It seemed unrealistic to think that we could have become friends, but I was lonely and had been willing to try.

A few days later, Dwayne came into my life. While sitting in the shade near the pool one afternoon, I noticed a man with long black hair wearing a leather vest sitting in a lawn chair not too far from me. As I watched him smoke and tie a bandana around his head, I wondered how he could sit in the hot sun. He must have heard my thoughts because he turned around and walked toward me.

"How you doin'?" he asked.

"You must be hot. I can barely sit under this umbrella in the shade," I said.

"Mind over matter, just used to it, I guess," he replied.

We made small talk about our jobs and I learned that he drove a van and delivered food and other items. As he talked I noticed the many tattoos that covered his arms and most of his neck. On each finger of both his hands he had letters and symbols.

"I like the tats on your hands," I said.

"Oh these," he said, pointing to his hands. "My bike club marks, lets us know our family when we're out and about."

Dwayne and I regularly met at the pool after work and talked about our day and our lives. I learned that he was working at the resort on a parole work program. However, he never told me what landed him in jail. It had something to do with his motorcycle gang, as he was not allowed to ride while on probation.

Once Dwayne and I became friends, the constant nighttime banging on my door and lewd comments stopped. Built like a truck, he didn't look like someone that you would want to get angry.

One night he asked me if I wanted to take a drive into town with him and a friend. I agreed, and as we drove down the highway, I learned that the plan was to buy beer and travel to Key West and spend the night. As he said this, my gut flashed an intuitive red flag and a feeling of dread crept up my spine. If there is one thing that I had learned, it was to trust these intuitive warnings. When I told him that I had to work the next morning and would like to go back to the club, he didn't argue and he drove me back.

The next day at work one of the managers tensely grilled me with questions about Dwayne.

"When was the last time you saw him? Where was he headed?"

Eventually I learned that the car he was driving was not

his and the police were looking for him. Although I never saw Dwayne again, he would soon play a part in an extraordinary encounter.

Fire and Water

For the next couple of months I settled into a comfortable rhythm. After work, I usually went to a secluded cove and swam. Lying in the sun and relaxing, I listened to the familiar and comforting whispers of my spirit friends. There was so much that I was grateful for. The odds that I could have gotten through all that I had recently experienced safely were pretty low. I knew that my spirit friends were guiding and watching out for me. They sent people to watch over me, and although I was alone and not sure where I was going and what to do next, I felt a sense of peace.

On my way back to my room around sunset one evening, I noticed a couple of fire trucks in the street near my building. As I got closer I saw smoke billowing from my window and fire hoses drenching everything inside. About an hour later I was allowed to collect my belongings. Everything was either soaked or destroyed by fire. Fortunately, I had opened a bank account to save the money I made waitressing. Although it looked as if the fire was started by faulty electrical wiring I was told that I had to leave. I didn't argue, but took it as a sign that it was time to return to school. The next day I was on a bus for the three-day ride up north.

Part III The Spirits Are Full of Surprises

Chapter 12

Ghosts from the Past

The sunlight shining down through the grimy bus windows was warm and relaxing. As we got closer to Massachusetts, tulips, pansies and crocus dotted the light-green grassy landscape. After getting off the bus, I headed to a used clothing store as I had almost nothing left after the fire. Then I went in search of my friends. Fortunately, I was invited to spend a few nights at the first door that I knocked on. Within a few days I found a small apartment to rent and work at a farm.

One Saturday while walking through a small park near the center of town I heard my name called. The voice sounded familiar, and when I turned to see who it was, I froze. With a smile and a wave, Bob my stepfather walked toward me.

In his best camp counselor voice he said, "How about lunch? I'd like a chance talk to you. There are some things I need to tell you."

I had no desire to see or talk to Bob, but I was curious. Despite my apprehension, I agreed and we walked to a restaurant I frequented.

After ordering a fried fish sandwich, I asked him how he knew where to find me.

"Your brother told me where you were living," he said.

"What do you want?" I asked.

He stirred his coffee, talked to the waitress, then said, "I've been in an intense kind of therapy and learned a lot. I know what I did to you was wrong and I want to apologize."

Not wanting to make eye contact, I watched the waitress as she wiped the counter. I wondered if this was another one of his games; he could be convincing. Skeptical and unsure of what to do, I didn't say anything. We sat in silence and ate for a few minutes.

Finally I said, "I'm glad you've been in therapy."

"It's been difficult, but good for me. I know you probably don't trust me. I'll give you my address and phone number," he said.

I think he knew that I wasn't going to give him my contact information and he didn't ask.

"Do you need anything?" he asked.

"I'm fine," I said.

He slid a couple of folded twenty dollar bills my way and I just stared at them.

"I don't talk to my mother much. I'm not going to try and help you get back together with her," I said.

He said nothing and we headed for the door. On the street, I thanked him for lunch and walked away.

"How about we do this again," he yelled. "I'll be up this way the last Saturday of the month about this same time. Meet me here for lunch?"

I said nothing and kept going.

Confused and not sure what to make of this unexpected visit, I walked until the sun set. My spirit friends were not much help. Instead of warning me away from him, they whispered encouragement.

"We helped send him your way," I heard.

"Why?" I asked.

I received no clear answer. My guides often pushed me beyond my comfort zone but this seemed a little too much.

The last Saturday of the month I hung around the park waiting to see if he showed up. When I saw him round the corner to the restaurant I followed him. From outside the restaurant window I watched him sit down in the same booth. A twinge of energy pushed me and I went in and sat across from him.

"Hi, I didn't think you would show up. Come on, take a seat," he said.

I sat down and said nothing.

"I attended a few primal scream therapy workshops. They are powerful. You just let out all of your deep feelings and tension. I've also taken up Zen meditation and I've been learning more about Eastern philosophy and spirituality," he said.

He then described what he called a breakthrough in consciousness that he had experienced in meditation.

I didn't quite know why he was telling me all of this, but I listened. Still suspicious of his motives, I didn't share much about myself or the psychic experiences that were increasingly consuming more and more of my time and energy.

Chapter 13

In the Flow of Precognition

Soon after reconnecting with Bob, I ran into an old friend who lived in the apartment next to mine during my first semester in college. We stopped to say hello and he introduced me to the long blond-haired friend that he was with. His friend had a rugged look to him and I immediately noticed that on each of his fingers he had the same tattoos that Dwayne my friend from Florida had.

"I had a friend in Florida with the same tats on each of his fingers," I said.

"What's his name?" he asked.

"Dwayne," I replied.

His eyes lit up and he said, "Oh yeah, dark hair, thick build, right?"

"That sounds like him," I said.

"That's wild, we used to ride together in Florida. Moved back up here to help my mother. I'm Larry. Wow, nice to meet you. How's Dwayne doing?"

"We worked at the same yacht club," I said. Then without giving it a thought I blurted out, "He drowned. Went to Key West one weekend and never saw him again."

"Oh, man, I'm so sorry to hear this. What a great guy, always there when you needed him," Larry said.

Before he could say anything else, I said, "Nice to meet you." Then quickly walked away.

When I turned the corner, I went into an alley and tried to catch my breath. Flushed and embarrassed, I couldn't believe what I had just said. As far I knew, Dwayne hadn't drowned and it made no sense for me to blurt this out.

The next day I went up into the mountains and sat by the

river. Between meeting Bob and lying to Larry, I had to figure some things out. It was late spring and the river was swollen from recent rains and the melting snow of the higher hills. It was an unusually warm day, and the birds, butterflies and bees all seemed happy and busy. It felt like a perfect day. As the swollen river moved around boulders and rocks in a deafening rumble, I took out my journal and began to write. Without giving it too much thought I wrote a long poem about someone getting pulled into a whirlpool and leaving the body behind for the light. After rereading the poem, I remembered what I told Larry the day before about Dwayne drowning. Something really is wrong with me, I thought.

Later the next day, I shared with a friend that I had gone up to the river the day before.

"You know someone drowned up there. Did you see anyone?" she asked.

"I went to my regular spot that's pretty secluded. Didn't see anyone. Who drowned?"

"Not sure, some guy," she said.

In search of answers, I bought a newspaper and a few pages in I saw a headline about the drowning. The man who drowned was Larry who I met two days' prior. Later that day I learned that a group of guys were up at the river drinking. Not realizing the strength of the current, Larry jumped off a high boulder into the river. He went under and never came up. After searching for him, his friends found his lifeless body up against a rock down river.

Although I was familiar with the spirit realm and psychic experiences, this felt different. I couldn't help but wonder if there was something more that I might have been able to do to prevent Larry's drowning. Instead of making up a story about our mutual friend drowning, maybe I could have warned him. The day and close to the same time of his accident, I wrote a poem about a man drowning in a whirlpool; maybe this was another message that I ignored.

Distraught and confused, I asked my guides for help.

"There was nothing more that you could do. Larry's passing had nothing to do with you. You are psychic and we wanted to motivate you," they said.

I had no idea what this meant. "Motivate me for what?" I asked.

"To know yourself."

My relationship with my spirit guides could be both enchanting and frustrating. Their agenda was not always what I expected or wanted it to be. As my psychic experiences intensified, my concerns and questions were not always answered to my satisfaction.

Instead of advice and guidance I was often told to, "focus more on the lessons and tap into my power and potential."

However, I didn't always know what that meant.

As much as I wanted to pull in the reins of my psychic awareness and take some time to figure some things out, it continued to march on unabated. Soon after Larry's passing, I began to have nightly dreams of Bob's grandmother. When I first met her she was in her late eighties and still kept up a garden, and walked up and down the narrow basement stairs to do laundry. She rarely spoke to me, but one day told me how she had fled Germany as Hitler rose to power.

"I was just a child and on the last boat out," she said. Then followed this up by telling me, "You need to get a job, don't be lazy."

In the dreams she was wearing the silver blue dress that she had made years earlier for her burial. It hung on her closet door so no one would forget. Each night I saw her in this dress walking. Then one night I dreamt that she walked through the gates of a cemetery. The next day, as I was sitting in my apartment's sunny kitchen, a blue and silver streak of color appeared and then floated out through the window. I knew that this was her spirit and that she had died. I was surprised, but felt honored that she came to say good-by. A day later there was a message waiting for me at my job from Bob, letting me know she had died.

Although my experience of her passing over was gentle, I couldn't help but wonder why I was psychically aware of people dying. Between Elvis Presley, Larry and now Bob's grandmother, there seemed to be a pattern. As much as I wanted to get on with the business of working and going back to school, the constant parade of psychic impressions was overwhelming. I felt and knew too much about things that I had no control over and could not change. I wanted to turn off my psychic awareness, but had no idea how to do this.

One day while listening to my sociology teacher expound on one of his more radical ideas, I decided to confide in him. A smallish thin man with a blond curly afro and bright blue eyes, he was the most open-minded teacher I ever had. After class I nervously approached his desk.

Stuffing papers into a stained leather bag, he looked up and asked, "What can I do for you?"

"You seem to know a lot about different things," I replied.

"I would like to think I do."

"Do you know anything about being psychic?" I asked.

Not looking too interested in our conversation, he said, "Why do you ask?"

"Well, I've had some experiences and don't know what to do or who to talk to about this," I said. "The last person I told was a priest and he thought I was crazy."

"I see, hmm… I find it all fascinating, wish I could help you. I guess my best advice would be to talk to someone else who is psychic or has had paranormal type experiences," he said.

"Good advice, thanks," I said and walked out to the hallway.

"At least he didn't think I was nuts. Now if I could just find someone who is psychic," I thought.

Chapter 14

Psychics Lend a Helping Hand

My search for a psychic who gave readings seemed futile. I searched for ads in free newspapers, bulletin boards and in bookstores, but came up short. One afternoon while visiting friends at the Quaker farm school where my old roommate had gone to high school, the director approached me.

"Nice to see you. Do you have a minute, there's something I want to run by you? We are all going out to Northern California to spend a few weeks in the forest. I'll be in the bus with the students, but I'd like to have my car while there. Would you be willing to drive it out for me?" he asked.

His request felt like the answer to my prayers. California seemed like the perfect place for me to meet psychics and learn from them. A month or so later, I stuffed some of my things into my backpack and got behind the wheel of his red compact car. Two students who I needed to take to Santa Monica accompanied me on the four-day drive.

Everything went smoothly, and after dropping off the students, I went in search of a psychic. It took four days to drive to California and ten minutes to find a psychic. In a free newspaper I found laying on a lunch counter, I noticed an announcement advertising a psychic fair that evening.

The hotel banquet room where the psychic fair was held was just a few miles away. I was waiting at the door when it opened. In a dimly-lit room, around a dozen or so small tables, sat psychics, card readers, healers and mediums. As I scanned the room, I was drawn to a dark-haired woman who looked a little out of place. Compared to some of the other participants who wore colorful flowing dresses or had crystals, new-age type statues or incense on their tables, she sat quietly behind a plain white cloth.

When my turn came for a reading, I sat across the table from her and she began to speak in a low soft voice. I was so excited I could barely focus, and by the time I settled down, it was over. On my way out of the hotel, I stopped in the restroom. As I washed my hands the psychic who I had just left came in and approached me.

"Where do you live?" she asked.

"In Massachusetts, I'm just passing through the area."

She continued to stare at me and said, "I'd like to work with you and help you to develop your gifts. You have a lot of psychic potential."

"Thank you, but I'm leaving tonight," I said and rushed out the door.

My head was spinning and I felt out of breath. Someone had acknowledged my psychic abilities, a psychic no less. Yet instead of feeling comforted and acknowledged, I became anxious and couldn't get away fast enough.

The Spiritualist Church

After dropping off the car in Northern California, I made my way by bus to San Francisco. There was not much to go back to in Massachusetts and I thought I would try to find a job and stay awhile. A friend of mine from high school had joined the military and was stationed in San Francisco and generously agreed to let me stay with her.

The day after I arrived I managed to figure out how to get downtown by bus and streetcar, and my job search began. Day after day I scanned the ads and walked the downtown streets filling out applications. One afternoon, I turned down a street that was a little quieter and less busy than most. I paused for a moment and noticed that I was standing in front of an older white storefront with a sign that read *Spiritualist Church All Welcome* on it. Although I had never been to a spiritualist church, I knew that they believed in communication with spirits. Delighted by this unexpected find, I took note of the time of their next service and navigated my way back to the bus stop.

Two days later, I got to the church just as the service was beginning. The room was full and I slipped into an empty folding chair in the back of the room. As I listened to the speaker, a woman came by and handed me a slip of paper and a small pencil. I had no idea what to do with it. She must have noticed the perplexed look on my face, because she told me this was a billet. If I wrote something on it, she would add it to the basket and I might get a message from one of the readers. I didn't know what to write so I drew a yin-yang sign, folded the paper and put it in the basket.

When the minister finished speaking we sang a song and then it was time for readings. An older slim man dressed in a black suit stood up and went to the podium with the help of a cane. He picked up a slip of paper and gave a message to the person whose billet he held. When he finished he called out the name on the billet and a woman in the audience thanked him and seemed quite happy.

He did this a few more times, then picked up another billet and said, "This will be the last one for today."

Closing his eyes, he said, "This person is very psychic and is going to have a unique ministry."

He went on to describe a future of communicating with the other side, healing, speaking, teaching and writing. I looked around the room wondering who he was talking to and noticed that others looked as if they were doing the same thing. When he finished, he opened the billet and held up the yin-yang symbol. I raised my hand to identify that this was mine and thanked him. On the way out of the church, the woman who had given the talk met me at the door. "We have psychic development class here on Wednesday evening," she said. "I'll see you then."

I walked out into the noisy San Francisco sunshine, elated but also confused. Despite the positive and affirming message that I had just been given, I was distrustful and even skeptical. Maybe they told this to everyone, I thought. I felt exposed, vulnerable but also elated. A part of me wanted to shout from the rooftops, *I'm not crazy, I'm psychic!* Another part of me wanted to find a good hiding place.

On Wednesday I attended the development class and began to learn how to corral my wild and unpredictable psychic energy. The class was taught by the woman minister who led the service and another woman who didn't speak English well, but nodded and smiled a lot. There were about a dozen other students of all ages and we sat in the same metal chairs and room where the service was held. We faced a wall that was filled with pictures of Jesus and angels and there were lit candles on a long table near the podium. The old wooden floor creaked a lot and I wondered if there were spirits walking around. We began the class by praying and asking God to protect and watch over us. The minister then asked for someone who had a question or concern to come and sit in front of the class.

A woman who looked to be in her early thirties quickly got up and took a seat in front of us. We were then instructed to close our eyes and receive a message for her. Several minutes later the minster told us that it was time to share what we received. As we went around the room, everyone had something different to say. Some seemed more confident than others, and the minister just nodded her head without giving any feedback and went to the next person. When it came my turn, I described an image in which I saw the woman with her head tilted to the side looking at a brown-haired man. Around her neck was a tight red scarf that didn't look very comfortable. The image was tense and it felt as if the woman wanted to say something to the man but was holding back. When I finished sharing, the minister looked at the woman with raised eyebrows. Then class was over. There was no feedback or help in interpreting or understanding what was received.

The following week, I got to class early. There was just one other student there, an older man with a British accent. In the first class I noticed that he held a small clear crystal orb in his hand which he continuously looked at.

He approached me with a smile and said, "How do you like class so far?"

"It's great," I said.

"You did good last week," he said.

"Really? I didn't know if what I saw meant anything. I still don't," I said.

Lowering his voice and looking around to make sure no one was listening, he said, "The woman who you were giving the message to is married to the minister's son. You described him in the vision you saw. The red scarf around her neck is a symbol of anger or strong emotions. The two of them were in some kind of spat and that is what her question was about."

"Oh, I see. Is that what you intuitively received?" I asked.

He laughed and said, "That comes to me by way of gossip... Take the time to understand and learn more about symbolism. A lot of psychic impressions come through this way."

The room was filling and we took our seats.

Similar to the first class we practiced tuning into a volunteer and this time the teacher gave some instruction on how to interpret what we received. Spurred on by what I was learning in class, I practiced interpreting the images and visions and listened within for more psychic insights, feelings and thoughts.

It felt as if a weight was falling off of me. The stress of feeling isolated and alone in my psychic world was lessening. In the past year I felt overwhelmed by an increase in psychic experiences. It felt as if I was living in two worlds, yet a stranger in both. The opportunity to bond and learn from others who had similar experiences helped me more than I had imagined it could.

Unfortunately I was running out of money. My job search

was challenging and I spent most of my time on buses going from place to place filling out applications. This was before cell phones and the Internet, and I didn't have a way for people to contact me. Along with these obstacles, I was not yet twenty-one and not legally allowed to work anywhere that sold liquor. After five weeks of job hunting I knew I had to return to Massachusetts. A friend who had been collecting my mail let me know that I received the school grant and financial aid which I had applied for several months earlier. Although I wanted to stay in San Francisco, I took this as a sign that I was meant to return to school.

However, it wasn't easy to leave the church. It had been a relief to go to the classes and services, and be seen and known and not feel judged. The part of me that believed that others would think I was crazy or delusional if they knew about my psychic inclinations relaxed and loosened its grip.

Although I was willing to go back to the Northeast, I was disappointed in myself for not being able to find work. The feeling that I was still on the outside looking in continued to haunt me. My guides in their characteristically positive way encouraged me to view my time in San Francisco as a successful adventure. Either way, I was back on a bus headed across the country.

Chapter 15

A Religion of Love and Poverty

It took five days and nights for the Greyhound bus to make its way across the country. Except for the occasional crying child or a few loud-talking passengers, the ride was peaceful. I shared pleasantries with whoever sat next to me and a few took the opportunity to fill me in on their personal issues and worries. However shallow or in depth our encounter was, my intuition filled me in on their thoughts, experiences, feelings, disappointments and hopes. Each passenger was a private universe. In my mind's eye I saw the burdens that a middle-aged Hispanic woman carried on her shoulders. When a young man dressed in army fatigues sat next to me I felt and saw a dense knot of pain lodged in his heart. Whatever he witnessed while in active duty clung to him and wouldn't let go. Others felt more hopeful and positive and their energy glowed like Christmas lights. The excited attractive dark-haired woman on her way to meet her boyfriend would soon be engaged and I felt her coming joy.

The Greyhound bus became a mini psychic laboratory, and as I tuned into others, little buds of compassion began to spontaneously sprout in my heart. I wanted to reach out and tell a mother who was concerned about her son that everything would work out, and let an older man know that his wife on the other side was with him. But, I stayed quiet, kept what I received to myself and gazed out the window.

When I got back to Massachusetts, I found another small, cheap apartment and attempted to settle into school and another job cleaning offices at the college. In my free time, I read and studied the spiritual books that I discovered in the used bookstores in San Francisco. Drawn to Eastern spiritual practices, like Buddhism and Taoism, I read everything I could about spiritual deities, gods, goddesses and other spiritual beings. Although I found no solace in organized religion, spirituality felt natural and easy to relate to. However, my perception of Christianity was about to be challenged.

It felt as if I was finally settling into school and work, but the spirits had a different plan. One morning the director of the Quaker farm showed up at my door and by the look on his face I knew he had another favor to ask of me.

After thanking me for driving his car to California, he said, "Would you be interested in helping an older woman? For years she rescued sick cats from the streets of New York City and took them to her home in Maine. She has well over a hundred cats. Legal action was taken against her in the town where she lives and she was given a choice to either get rid of the sick cats or move. She chose to move and we offered to give her temporary sanctuary and found a more long-term situation for her in upstate New York, at a Catholic Worker Farm. However, we need someone to help get her there."

"How would I get her there?" I asked.

"She's got an old truck and she built a container on the bed where she keeps the cats," he said. "She can't drive it though. It's a bit old."

"When?" I asked.

"That's the thing, she came in yesterday and has to be gone by the time students come back from winter break," he said.

The next day I went up to the farm to meet her. When I walked into the kitchen, I saw an older woman staring into her coffee cup. With long thin white hair and a small frame, she looked to be in her late seventies or eighties. Her light blue eyes looked a little blurry and she had a worried look on her face.

I introduced myself as the person who would be driving her to New York.

"Call me the cat lady," she said. "I need to get my cats to a safe place as soon as possible. When can we leave? Can we go tomorrow?"

I did my best to assure her that I would help.

"We need to go right away," she said. "Follow me."

Without looking back she led me to one of the barns. We went in a side door, and when I saw a mid-1950s red pickup with a tall makeshift plywood box built onto the bed, I almost changed my mind. The truck was in poor condition, rust covered the bottom and the tires were so old they looked like they could have been the original ones. It looked as if any minute the truck and the cat box might fall apart. I had never driven a vehicle with this kind of transmission and I was skeptical of my ability. I told her my concerns and she let out a deep long wailing cry. I didn't know what to do and just stared at her.

She finally stopped to catch her breath. Then yelled in a high-pitched voice, "The cats have been confined to this plywood box for a week! The farm will not let me take them out!"

With tears in her eyes, she continued, "They're going to die. We have to leave right now, tonight!"

I told her I could leave in a couple of days. She looked down at the snow and started to walk away.

"Okay, I'll take you tomorrow," I said.

Without turning around, she said, "You better."

The next day was Christmas and I had planned on having a quiet day. Instead I got a few things together and walked up to the farm early in the morning. The cat lady was waiting for me, and as soon as she saw me, she got in the truck. It had snowed during the night and the roads had a coating of snow and ice. Still there was no turning back. As I drove down the mountain with a truckload of sick cats watching the plywood shelter shift with every turn, I wondered how I would ever make the six-hour drive. The truck's top speed was forty miles an hour so I took a slower back road route. We made frequent stops to check on her cats and against all odds finally arrived at the farm as the sun was setting.

As I drove down the long snow-piled driveway to the farm, I noticed several cabins and a tall older five-story brick building with a tall watchtower. The farm bordered the Hudson River and spread out over many acres. There were a few people going in and out of a large white two-story building, so I parked next to it. While the cat lady checked on her cats, I went in the front door and was met by a middle-aged woman who seemed happy to see me. She said that they had been expecting us and our timing was perfect as dinner was about to be served. As we walked to the dining hall, a few people silently sat in old stuffed chairs and couches. None of the furniture matched and the room had no rugs or pictures on the walls or other furnishings. In the dining room there was an odd assortment of tables and chairs, and people were lining up at near a long table filled with food.

I was immediately struck by the diversity of those gathered for the Christmas meal. There were older people who needed help getting their food, children laughing and playing, and a woman who seemed to be carrying on a conversation with herself. Slowly, more people wandered in including a couple who could not speak English and a few hippy types. There was an Amish man dressed in a black suit and top hat who I later learned had walked there with his goat from Pennsylvania. In a darkened corner there was a small group of serious-looking people of all ages who appeared to be praying.

Peggy, the woman who greeted me at the door, sat with me while I ate. Her greying blond hair was held back with a hairband and she wore a heavy dark winter sweater, a skirt and knee socks.

"There is a cabin close to the main road that the cat lady can stay in. How long will you be visiting?" she asked.

"Not long, is there someone who can drive me to the closest bus station?" I asked.

"Oh, please consider staying as long as you would like. We

are just so happy to have you. There is a room here in the main building where you can stay."

She seemed genuinely pleased that I was there. Watching the odd array of people in the dining hall, all celebrating Christmas together, warmed my heart. I was grateful that I was there.

The next morning I got up early and began to explore the sprawling estate. Although it was aged and in need of repairs, it was still impressive. In addition to the main house there were a dozen or so cabins scattered throughout the hills and woods and an old brick building that had an expansive view of the Hudson River and surrounding valley. There were chicken coops, a large barn, and beyond the woods, farmland. The scent of burning wood and the dancing sunlight on the river created an almost surreal atmosphere.

As I stood on the porch taking it all in, a pretty woman with long auburn hair, and three blond-haired girls in tow, came toward me.

"Hi, my name is Beatrice," the woman said. Pointing to her girls who all appeared to be under six, she said, "This is River, Lakeshia and Willow. We saw you come in yesterday and wanted to say hello."

After exchanging pleasantries, I turned to Beatrice.

"I've never been anyplace like this. Is this run by the Catholic Church?"

She laughed. "No, this isn't really a church thing, there's no government or church money. We only accept private donations."

She must have noticed my perplexed look and continued. "Dorothy Day, the founder, lives in the city in a shelter for women and children. She's more of a radical Catholic, she's been arrested for civil disobedience and for many years was a socialist. She started the Catholic Worker in the late 1930s, I think. All the people you see here have no other place to go. Most were living on the street in New York and went to the soup kitchens that Dorothy started. She bought the farm to grow food for the homeless in the city and then invited the longer-term homeless to come live here."

Beatrice's daughters, who had been kicking snow off the porch, were now trying to break off a long icicle hanging over the edge. We walked down the steps toward the brick building where she lived with her husband and the kids.

"How does everything get done, like the cooking and farming?" I asked.

"Not sure, it just somehow does or it doesn't, no one is expected to work if they can't. Sometimes people come up from the city and volunteers show up from all over. We really do live on faith. Nice to meet you, I've got to get my daughters inside," she said.

As I watched her pick up one of her daughters and shoo the other two inside, it struck me that maybe I felt comfortable here because I knew what was like to live on the fringe and barely get by. This wasn't like the Christianity that I was familiar with. Instead of rules and judgment, there seemed to be acceptance and compassion. I wanted to know more about this place, the people and the intangible something that I felt tugging at my heart since I arrived.

Initially I was only going to be there for a day or two. However, there was something present, an energy, a spiritual presence perhaps that quietly and soothingly filled in the cracks and holes of the damaged and broken lives of the residents. Despite the sparse surroundings, the ill health of many of the residents and the meals that mostly consisted of beans, rice and cornbread, this was not a sad place. Like a beam of sunlight escaping the clouds, compassion spread its rays of warmth. I wanted and needed to be part of it, if only for a few more weeks.

In the days that followed, I painted the dining room and helped out in the kitchen and put my dishwashing skills to use. The residents were friendly and liked to talk about their lives before they came to the farm. The difficulties and suffering they endured helped me to put my own troubles into perspective. Most had no family and had lived on the streets of New York City for years. As they talked I felt their loneliness and allowed my own experience of being cast aside to be acknowledged. Quite often I saw and felt the presence of their loved ones who had passed over hovering close to them. I wanted to share this and let them know the love that the spirit realm was sending to them, but I resisted and said nothing.

A few weeks after arriving I headed back to school.

Chapter 16

The Big Letting Go

Back in my apartment I continued to work and go to classes. As the end of the school year approached I felt more and more unsettled. I was attending a two-year school and it was time to make some decisions about the future. My job cleaning offices was also ending, and without a car for transportation, I was having a difficult time finding another one. As money became tighter and without a job in sight, I turned to my spirit guides for direction. As soon as I sent my request their way, I saw an image of a tent near the Mohawk River.

When I was young we often went camping in the mountains along the river. This is where I first met my Native American guide, Tetchuwatchu. One morning I had gotten up early and went alone to the river, which I was not supposed to do. Near a big boulder I saw the outline of a tall man with a long braid. His hands were on his hips and he was smiling at me. Then he was gone. A few days later, I caught a glimpse of him in the woods and again he quickly disappeared. This happened a few more times until one day I asked him who he was. Immediately I heard Tetchuwatchu. It took me many years to realize that in his name was the message of his purpose, Teach you, watch you.

The Mohawk River wound through the mountains not far from where I lived. The tourist season brought in more people and I would likely be able to get work at a park. Without having to pay rent, I could save money if I lived at a campground. However, I had no camping equipment, no car to get there and didn't quite know how to make it work.

Around this time, I received a postcard from Bob letting me know that he was coming up to my area. Although I had not seen him in several months, I had a post office box where he occasionally sent me mail. In the postcard he asked me to meet him at the diner for lunch. A couple of weeks later I sat in a booth and waited for him feeling a little desperate. I couldn't afford the next month's rent on my apartment and didn't know where I was going.

After waiting a few minutes, I began to think that seeing him again was not a great idea. I got up to leave and saw him walking toward me.

We made small talk while I ate a fish sandwich and a big pickle.

As our conversation dwindled to silence he asked me, "Is there anything that I can help you with?"

In the past I had said no and that ended the conversation. This time I had a different answer.

"I need a tent and a sleeping bag," I said.

"Why, are you going camping?"

"I am thinking of camping up on the Mohawk Trail and getting a job doing grounds work or something at one of the campgrounds."

He looked at me for a minute. Then said, "Okay, we can go to a sports store when we are done here. There's one on the road I came in on."

A week later Bob loaded my camping equipment into his blue compact car and drove me up the mountain. We found a small private campground that was going to be closed for the season, however, they agreed to let me stay and help out. It was early spring and still a little chilly, especially at night. My tent was close to the river and the continuous sound of water flowing over the rocks and boulders was soothing and almost hypnotic. I felt absorbed into the beauty. As the trees, flowers and other vegetation came to life, it felt as if my soul was being renewed and restored. There was a small bus that traveled along the mountain route once a day. If I needed food, I went to the street and waved and they picked me up.

When not working clearing brush, I hiked, sat next to the river, meditated and eased into an intimate and comfortable connection with my spirit friends. There were other new spirits, mostly Native American, that I caught glimpses of in the woods and near the river. Blue jays also seemed to take an interest in me. About three of them came and went from their perch in the trees above my tent. Wherever I went I saw them close by. One day I took the bus to town to do some shopping. When I got back I noticed that the clay sun that I hung from the top of my tent was turned around. It felt as if this meant something, but I didn't know what. In the sky above me the blue jays were circling and making quite a racket. I turned my head up to watch and intuitively listen to them and immediately became aware that someone had been there to see me. About a week later, I went to town again and bumped into a friend who told me that he had gone to my camp to say hello, but I wasn't there. When I found out that he had gone up to see me on the same day that I had gone to town, I thanked the blue jays for watching out for me.

For several weeks I enjoyed the gentle rhythm and beauty of the river and being closer to the spirits. Then one morning a truck came barreling down the dirt path almost knocking down my tent. A man who I recognized as the owner of the property clumsily got out of his truck.

"Sorry about that, I came a little close there," he said. "I hate to have to ask you to leave, but the family wants to get going on some plans to build a cabin, right about here. Thought we had more time, but they're anxious. Gonna get started as early as next week."

My heart sank. I had hoped to be there longer and I had no place to go. For a moment I thought of taking my tent and moving deeper into the woods. However, I knew that it was time to leave. That night after a fitful sleep, I woke up before dawn and went and sat near the river. As the sun slowly rose it illuminated the sparkling mist rising from the humming water.

In this soft peace, I thought about my options.

The obvious choice was to move to a more populated area to find work and continue with school. But there was no place that I wanted to go and I wasn't too excited about getting another cleaning or waitress job. Then there was school. I wanted to get my degree, but I wasn't sure what I wanted to study.

As I sat and watched the sun peek up above the distant mountains, different future scenarios played out in front of me. I saw myself moving back to the town where I grew up, reconnecting with friends and getting a job. Images of attending a four-year college and becoming a teacher, a social worker or a nurse paraded in front of me. I saw myself eventually marrying and living my life out. Yet in each of these different paths, the outcome was the same. I saw myself older, sitting next to the river and confronting the same question that had always plagued me.

Why am I here? What is my reason for being?

From the pit of my stomach a deep loneliness made its way to the surface. It was a hollow vacancy that I had always known and didn't think I could ever escape from. I was here in this world, but I couldn't find my place. There was a depth and emptiness in being alone and feeling a stranger in the world with no home. Out of step and balancing on the fringe, it felt as if I was continually trying to make my way and figure everything out. My heart and soul wanted to be free, to sail unencumbered in the sky with the spirits. I knew this was unrealistic but I couldn't fully embrace the expectations and demands of a purely material existence either.

The spirits were my family, my mother and father and my friends. I didn't want to go into the world and lose this connection. More than a sentimental attachment, this was my reality. It was within the marrow of my bones, in my heart and soul. This was all I had and I wouldn't give it up.

As I sat on a cold boulder damp from the morning mist, a blue jay flew by and landed on a branch so close to me, I could have touched him. I stared at him and he stared back at me.

"What do I do?" I asked him.

From somewhere deep in my heart a feeling and awareness started to surface. In a moment of crystalized realization the air and everything around me seemed to pause. I realized that I didn't have to figure all of this out. All of the different options, plans and dreams of who or what I could be were meaningless. This awareness did not come from a sense of depression, weariness or stress, but from my heart and soul knowing. As this truth came to light I felt the heaviness and burdens drop away. A shiver of energy moved through me and I felt different, like something finally made sense.

I looked at the beauty that surrounded me and the sun rising higher into the sky, and I knew what I needed and wanted to do. I was ready to fully give my life away; I didn't want it.

For as long as I could remember there was a spiritual presence close to my side. It was always there and at the same time it was out of my reach and understanding. Whatever this was, I was ready to let go into this spiritual atmosphere, energy and presence. The knowing and love that I had always felt was not of this world and I offered my life to it. I finally felt free and I said out loud:

My life is your life, take it and do with it what you will. Wherever you want me to go, I will go. Whatever you want me to do or be, I am yours.

Still watching me the blue jay spread its wings and took flight. As it did my spirit also lifted into freedom. I didn't have to figure it all out. I just had to listen to this ever-constant spiritual presence and follow where I was led. This was one thing that I thought I could be good at.

Part IV Is This Holiness?

Chapter 17

I am an Apparition

That illusive something that I felt at the Catholic Worker Farm pulled me to return. Having made the decision to surrender to the ever-present spiritual presence and allow it to guide me, I accepted the farm's intuitive invitation. However, I didn't know how I was going to get there. With no transportation to get to a bus station and with too much camping gear to hitchhike, I knew I had to ask for help from Bob. However, I didn't know his phone number or address.

With time running out, my spirit guides suggested I send Bob a telepathic message. This seemed like a long shot, but I was willing to give it a try. I knew he meditated in the early evening and this seemed like the best time to get his attention. After settling down next to the camp fire, I imagined an image of Bob and sent him the message that I needed him to come get me. In my mind's eye I saw myself get his attention and I continued to send him this message until I got drowsy and started to fall asleep.

Early the next morning while eating a hard bagel, I saw Bob's car wind down the road toward me. It felt both surreal and oddly normal that he got my message.

Halfway out of his car, and with a panicky look in his eyes, he asked me, "What's wrong? What's going on? I was meditating last night and I saw an image of you in the mirror. I felt that I needed to get here and find out what's going on; it felt urgent."

After I told him that I had to leave and that I sent him a telepathic message, he looked at me like he had just seen a ghost. In a way, I guess he had.

Although he agreed to take me to a bus station, he seemed disappointed in my decision to go back to the farm. He rattled off a number of reasons why I should get a job and go back to school instead. However, there was no changing my mind.

Farming

The next evening, I sat on the porch of a tiny cabin and stared into the woods. The cabin didn't have a kitchen or bathroom and there was just enough room for a chair and small table. A rickety ladder led to a sleeping loft that was buzzing with wasps who didn't seem too thrilled that I was there. I let them know that I wouldn't hurt them if they didn't hurt me and we managed to accommodate one another.

The following morning I made my way to the garden. Most of it had been planted. However, there was still a large section that was overgrown and needed work. The garden was large and I wondered who was doing the planting and other work. As I stood in the morning sun overwhelmed by the thought of tackling all the weeds, I heard the roar of an engine coming from the woods. Turing around I saw an old red tractor, that looked as if it was from another century, making its way toward me. An older man wearing a black baseball cap, and with a wild grin on his face, waved and drove past me in a cloud of dust. Later that afternoon on my way to the dining hall, I noticed him sitting outside of the barn. I introduced myself, and after stamping out his cigarette, he told me to call him Farmer Joe.

"Even when I lived on the streets, that's what people called me. Had my own farm long ago, crops went bad, I stared at the bottle most days and lost everything. Ended up going to the city, and when that didn't work out, I slept in the gutter. Dorothy took me aside at the soup kitchen one day and told me to get on up here and do some farming. Sure could use some help though, it's a big job," he said.

His watery grey eyes lit up when I told him I would be there the next day to give him a hand.

A few minutes later as I entered the dining room, I caught

a glimpse of a woman in flowing robes skirting through the kitchen. She moved quickly and then disappeared. Toby, an older man who lived in a cabin not too far from mine, noticed my curiosity.

"That's Ibis, she's an Egyptian goddess. I don't know if that's true or not, but she believes it," he said. "Says she lived around the time that the pyramids were built. Came back, not sure why. You won't see much of her. Stays in her room most of the time. Does some kind of magic. She's okay, nice lady."

The level of acceptance of one another's quirks and eccentricities was inspiring. Toby finished getting his meal of beans and vegetables and went to a corner table, looked out the window and began to talk to himself. It didn't appear as if I was the oddest person there and being psychic likely wouldn't ruffle any feathers.

A few weeks after my arrival at the farm, I noticed that my psychic ability seemed to be increasing. Maybe it was the open atmosphere at the farm or the interesting people and spirits by their side that amplified my intuitive receptivity. For whatever reason, more spirits seemed to reach out and want to talk to me.

For instance, the first time I saw Philip he was sitting on a folding chair on the spacious front lawn looking up at the sky. By his side was a female spirit surrounded by a glowing light. As I stood on the front porch looking at them both, he must have felt me staring as he turned and called to me.

"What you doin', girl? Come on over here."

A large man, in his fifties, Philip was well over six feet tall and could barely walk, even with the help of crutches.

"Don't be scared of me. Can't walk much, even with these crutches. I was born this way. Both my feet deformed from birth. Family didn't have enough money for surgery and I was a big boy. Mom couldn't carry me around and took me to a hospital. Only it was a mental hospital. Nothing wrong with my head though. They didn't figure that out until I was almost ten. Put me in an orphanage then. You know life gives you all kinds of things to deal with. Ended up living in the street. Had to beg for money while sitting on cardboard; I did better than most. People liked giving me money. Then along came Dorothy. Told me she had a good place for me and got me a ride up here. Best place I've ever been. I sit out in the sun looking at the clouds. This is how God talks to me," he said.

As he continued to talk, the female spirit behind him smiled and the gold light surrounding her seemed to get stronger. I felt her love and warmth and knew she was doing her best to watch out and take care of him. She let me know that she was his grandmother and had been watching over him since he was a child. I wanted to tell Philip about her, but I didn't know how to bring it up. I tried to turn the conversation to his family, but Philip just continued to talk and talk. When he paused for a moment, I said something about his family watching over him from heaven.

"Oh, I know that's true," he said. "Feel them with me, sometimes I see Jesus too. He's always with me."

It didn't appear that he needed my help.

Chapter 18

When the Spirit is Divine

Because of my experience with farm work, I spent most mornings working in the garden. I pulled weeds, tied up tomatoes and plucked off the bugs. Although there were other volunteers, few worked in the garden and most days I was the only one there.

About eight-thirty every morning a pale priest with thinning hair passed by the garden on the path that led from the small town to the main house. Catholic mass was held in the "chapel," which was really just a large room in the main house behind the kitchen. Although few attended, he showed up every day in his dark suit and white clerical collar. I usually greeted him with a wave and a hello. Although I had no fondness for religion and felt no desire to go to mass, his consistent presence got me thinking. Even though this was a Catholic Worker Farm there seemed to be very little of what I had come to think of as religious. No one ever mentioned God or asked me if I was Catholic or seemed to care. Grace was never said before meals, and with only a few random exceptions, I never saw anyone pray or read the Bible. Still, I was curious and decided to visit the chapel.

The following afternoon I ventured down the darkened hallway on the side of the kitchen that led to the chapel. The door was unlocked, and even though everyone was welcome, I felt like an intruder. The chapel was a little less dingy-looking than the rest of the house, and on the wall closest to the river, there was a tarnished metal crucifix. In front of it was a small wooden podium where I assumed the priest said mass. There were a few well-worn couches and overstuffed chairs with crocheted doilies on the armrests. Pictures of Mother Mary, Jesus and a few saints lined the walls. As I turned to leave, I noticed some shelves packed with dusty books near the door. As I looked through the aged hardcover books, I picked out a few and left.

Sitting on my porch later that day in the last light of the falling sun, I opened a book about saints and began to read. As I browsed through the chapters, I was surprisingly captivated. The stories of suffering, miracles, visions and other unexplained phenomena were nothing like the subdued and tame Christianity that I knew. The passion and fevered devotion of Saint John of the Cross and the visions and mystical experiences of Saint Teresa of Avila and Saint Catherine had me spellbound.

Night after night as I read about the saints, the unfamiliar spiritual presence that I felt since my arrival at the farm grew stronger. Although I had an intuitive sense of who this was, it felt outlandish to acknowledge her. A part of me felt like a hysterical mystic, dramatizing the invisible and spiritual. Yet, I knew this was Mary. I felt her everywhere, in the dining hall, the gardens, the fields, my cabin and by my side. However, instead of feeling comforted by this, I felt uneasy and couldn't understand why she was close. In the Protestant churches I attended, Mary was only spoken of at Christmas and this was as Jesus' mother. I didn't know Mary and wasn't comfortable with all that she represented.

However, my resistance didn't seem to matter. One night while walking through the woods to my cabin, I saw a shimmering outline of blue light in the meadow. In a momentary intuitive recognition, I felt Mary and my heart spontaneously opened with feelings of love. As quick as I saw and felt this apparition, I denied it. I told myself that this was just the light of the full moon and the glow of the stars reflecting against the summer dew. I wasn't ready to let go and allow whatever was happening to continue. Yet, despite my opposition, a powerful force was moving into my heart. I knew that my inner resistance and feelings of unworthiness wouldn't be able to keep it at bay for long.

After returning the books to the chapel, I decided to focus

more on the never-ending work that needed to be done on the farm. I gardened, ran errands for others in the old station wagon and tried out new recipes to be a more creative cook. Not interested in religion, I was happy with my familiar spiritual guides.

However, I continued to feel a persistent loving presence in my heart and couldn't help but wonder if this was Mary. A perplexing inner pressure was building within me and I didn't know what to do. Although I was comfortable with my connection and communication with the unseen, I found myself questioning what was real and what was illusion. Doubt began to plague me and I was having a difficult time understanding what was happening. While walking to the dining hall one morning it occurred to me to ask for a sign. Although it seemed a silly idea, I wanted some sense of assurance that I wasn't delusional.

"If all of this is real, Mary, if you are really with me, bring me a wooden cross by sunset," I said.

Although this felt like an unreasonable request, I knew it was possible. I would not seek out a cross or go in search of one, I told myself. Whatever happened I would take it as a sign and I didn't feel overly attached to an outcome.

Feeling a sense of relief, I continued my walk to the dining hall and after breakfast worked in the garden for most of the day. After dinner on my way to my cabin, I decided to say good-by to another volunteer who was getting ready to leave. He had been at the farm for several months and had decided to join a religious order and become a monk. His cabin was on the edge of a hill and had a great view of the river. As I approached I saw him on his porch, busy stuffing things into a backpack. We talked for a few minutes, and as I turned to go, he handed me a shoe box.

"I'm giving these things away. It's been pretty much picked through, just a couple of things left. Take whatever you would like," he said.

There were only two small items in the box. One of which was a wooden cross. I held it up against the background of the setting sun.

"I think this is for me," I said.

The odds of receiving a wooden cross while the sun was setting were pretty low. Despite this confirming sign of her presence, I still struggled to put aside my doubt. Instead of feeling blessed, I felt uncomfortable. I was not the picture of purity and innocence. All that I imagined Mary to be, I was not. Not pious or holy, I smoked, had hitchhiked many miles and could hold my own in most difficult situations. Not a fan of the church, I preferred being in the woods with my spirit friends. I couldn't imagine why she was close and what she wanted.

My thoughts quickly gave way to a flood of emotions. Despite my best attempts to push Mary's penetrating compassion and love away, I couldn't resist her. Little by little she chipped away at my heart. The hardened shell that surrounded me was no match for her power and I felt vulnerable and scared. Love was sweeping through me, and instead of bringing me peace it stirred up the long-buried pain of my childhood. Although Mary's love was soft and warm, it was also penetrating and a damn hard force to hold back. It called the dark emotions and memories out of their hiding place and it felt as if every emotion I had ever experienced was coming to the forefront. Tears flowed through me and I thought I might fall apart.

I still went to the garden every day and socialized with the other residents, but at night in my cabin, I felt as if I was being gutted. There was endless sorrow and I had no power to stop whatever process had taken hold of me. It was as if Mary's love was an elixir that pulled the pain out of me. I was humbled and felt like a little mouse in the midst of an immense and powerful force that I didn't understand.

Fortunately the process was swift. In about two weeks the intensity began to give way and an inner emptiness emerged.

The inner tension eased and I began to feel lighter and noticed beauty in the simple things around me. The plants in the garden, where I spent most of my time, were a source of strength and comfort. I felt the spark of life within them pushing through the dark soil seeking the sunlight. Despite the weeds, the heat and the poor conditions, the plants grew, blossomed and did their job. They produced and offered something of substance and beauty to the world. It was the simple joy of the emergence that they lived for. This is what it felt like for me. Something within me was pushing aside the darkness and fear, and reaching for the light.

Chapter 19

Another Saintly Visitor

While allowing a greater love and presence to fill me was challenging and difficult, loving others was easy. There were plenty of opportunities at the farm to freely give. Being with those in need offered relief and shifted my focus away from me. No matter how lousy and confused I felt, there was always someone on the farm who had it worse and was in pain. This put my personal challenges into perspective and I sought to be of service where and when I could.

However, I wasn't always confident in my ability to help others and provide what was asked of me. Late one night restless and unable to sleep, I went to the main house to get a cup of tea. As I was about to leave I saw Ed, an older man who had lived at the farm for several years, pacing in the front room. With a distressed look on his face, he rushed toward me.

"I need some help," he said. "Jerry, you may not know him, he's a new guy here. He just tried to cut himself with an old knife. It was so dull, not sure how much damage he could do with it. I found him curled up on the bathroom floor. He's okay, just a small nick. He's in the backroom. I stopped him, but I think he may try again. He's sick and depressed. Can you talk to him and pray with him?"

"I'm so glad you were there for him. I would like to help, but I'm not sure I'm the right person. Someone else might be better at this kind of thing," I said.

"Please, just talk to him," he said.

I followed Ed and found Jerry lying on a bed in a small cluttered room, smoking and staring into space. The thin blue blanket that covered him was littered with holes, and when he saw me, he slowly sat up. Unshaven and dirty, he was pale and thin and you could see his boney outline through his tee shirt. I sat on a partially rusted metal chair next to him and struggled to find the right words to say. As I witnessed his pain, my heart opened. He was ill but refused to go the hospital and told me he just wanted to be forgiven and to make himself right with God. I listened and talked to him, and most of the time we sat in silence. Overwhelmed by the intensity of his condition, I shed a few tears. After a while, the sun started to come up and he fell asleep.

On the way back to my cabin in the early morning mist, I saw the spirit of a nun on the path. She was young, wore a dark habit and smiled at me. Then she was gone. With no sleep the night before, I assumed I was in a dreamlike state and didn't think too much about it. However, a few days later while at work in the garden, I looked up and saw her again. She had a mischievous look on her face, then disappeared.

One evening after dinner I went back to the chapel to return the last book that I had borrowed. While there I noticed a small framed painting of a nun on a side table. She looked familiar and I realized that this was the nun that I saw on the path and in the garden. I picked up the picture and at the bottom of it was transcribed, The Little Flower. I didn't know what that meant or who she was. Determined to find out, I rummaged through the books until a small leaflet fell out of one. On it there was a picture of the young nun holding a bouquet of roses with the name St. Therese of Lisieux printed on it. After searching for more information about her, I found a small book that I took back to my cabin.

A few days later as rained poured through a small hole in my roof, I read about St. Therese or the Little Flower as she had come to be known. The more I learned about her, the more surprised I was that she had appeared to me. Unlike some of the more visionary and exotic saints, St. Therese was known for her love and unwavering devotion to Jesus. At the age of fifteen she petitioned the pope to allow her to be the youngest girl to enter a convent. He agreed and she became a Carmelite nun who welcomed suffering as a testament to her love of Jesus. She died at the age of twenty-four of tuberculosis. As much as I wanted to, I simply could not relate to her.

Confused as to why St. Therese was close, I thought that maybe her presence was an anomaly and she would not be back. However, not only did I soon see her again, her presence was stronger than ever.

Still dealing with the upheaval and effect that Mary's presence had on me, I was apprehensive about St. Therese's sudden appearance. Mary was a force. Like a strong ocean current or the wind blowing over a vast open plain, her love and spirit swept through me. So far I had not experienced St. Therese in this way, but I was bracing myself. I continued to catch glimpses of her, watching me and always smiling.

One day while working in the garden, I saw a faint image of her and asked her why she was with me.

"You've got the wrong person," I said. "I don't even know if I'm a Christian or want to be. I'm not really like you."

I didn't get a reply. A few days later she reappeared, still smiling. I didn't have discussions and interactions with her like I had with my other spirit guides and teachers. Instead she tugged at my heart, and despite my best attempts to remain detached, she made me smile. As with Mary, her love and compassion was irresistible, and yet, I didn't feel worthy. I didn't struggle with the idea that she was close, I was comfortable with seeing spirits. Instead it was the changes that both she and Mary seemed to invoke within me that were challenging.

It wasn't just the spirit world that circled my heart like a bird of prey. As I got to know the residents better and listened to their stories, I felt a compassion that surprised me. The farm housed the refuse from the streets, the truly poor and forgotten who slept in cardboard boxes in alleys and begged for food.

Most were old and suffered with mental and physical illness. Their suffering crept into my heart and soul. Eventually it was this inner ache that motivated me to reach out to Mary and St. Therese.

One morning during an unexpected cold spell in early fall, I went to the dining room for breakfast and noticed a woman pacing and agitated. She was smoking and talking to a few of the residents who were eating breakfast. I grabbed a coffee and sat down near them and noticed a little blond-haired girl who looked to be about three years old seated near the edge of the table. As I listened to the agitated woman talk, I realized this was the little girl's mother and they had recently been evicted from their apartment. They had no place to go and the mother was clearly not happy to be at the Catholic Worker Farm. As she continued to rant about her landlord, her boyfriend, and others, the little girl seemed unfazed. She picked at a biscuit and seemed to be in her own world. On her forehead there was a large dark and protruding birthmark and two fleshy nodules on one side of her nose. As I watched her and her mother, I realized the difficulties that this girl had yet to confront. Unless the birthmarks were expertly corrected she would no doubt struggle with her appearance. As her mother described, to no one in particular, the details of the fight she had with her landlord, it was clear that the little girl would have other issues to contend with as well.

After listening to the mother's long-winded tirade, I went up to the garden. However, I was unsettled and wanted to do something for her and especially the little girl. Yet, there seemed to be nothing I could do to help. Around lunch time, still feeling powerless, I stopped by my cabin and searched through my belongings. Through all my travels I had held onto a charm bracelet from my childhood. It was my only remaining item of any sentimental and material value.

As I sat holding it, I asked Mary and St. Therese to help the little girl.

"I'm okay, would you help her? She needs your love and comfort."

I didn't really expect an answer. Yet a rush of warmth filled my heart, along with the awareness that I could send this love to the little girl. I imagined that the bracelet could soak in Mary and St. Therese's love and that it would somehow help and bring comfort to the little girl.

When I entered the dining room a short time later, I was not too surprised to see the mother still pacing and smoking. The little girl was twirling in circles close by. After filling a plate with beans and rice, I sat close to them and took out the charm bracelet. I held it up to the mother and asked her if I could give this to her daughter. She looked surprised.

"Of course, you can," she said. "Crystal, come look at what this lady has for you."

I handed the bracelet to the little girl and she smiled and went back to twirling.

A few minutes later, one of the residents came in and told the mother that he could take her to the bus station. She gathered her things and they left.

Chapter 20

Shoes from an Angel

Despite the personal challenges and differences among the residents of the farm, it was a community of inclusive acceptance. Perhaps it was this open and nonjudgmental environment that motivated me to share a few of my psychic experiences with a few of the other volunteers. After listening to my nervous admission, they seemed unfazed and I began to receive requests for intuitive readings. My psychic ability had been dammed up inside me for a long time and it felt good to freely share and help others in this way.

However, I still had questions. Even though I knew that being psychic wasn't evil, I never thought of it as compatible with Christianity either. In the churches I grew up in I never heard the word psychic or anything close. It was no secret that most Christians didn't accept talking to spirits and other sixth sense phenomena. Although I was becoming more comfortable with my psychic ability and my connection to Mary and St. Therese, I still couldn't understand how it all fit together.

It helped that the farm didn't operate by status quo beliefs about religion, the material laws and limitations or anything else. Every day defied explanation. When there was no money to pay the bills, buy farm equipment or food, a large donation came in. A carload of children's clothing and bedding would be dropped off the day before a needy family arrived. A volunteer who could fix plumbing or electrical issues showed up when something broke. Miracles such as these were expected and the farm depended on them.

When I needed a pair of shoes, I experienced this type of miraculous manifestation. Although we regularly received donations of clothing and other useful items, shoes for my big feet were hard to come by. As an unpaid volunteer, I learned how to get by with little possessions and for months I had been wearing a pair of plastic flip-flops. It was getting cold and every day I checked the donations hopeful that shoes would show up.

On my way down the path to the dining hall early one morning, I encountered an older African-American man dressed in a dark suit and wearing shiny black shoes. Although it was unusual to encounter anyone on the path other than those who lived in the cabins, I had come to expect the unexpected. After exchanging a greeting, he asked me why I was wearing flip-flops.

"These are my only shoes," I said.

"A woman needs shoes," he said. "No worries, I'll get you a pair."

I laughed and said, "I've been waiting for some."

We then went our separate ways.

After breakfast I did some cleaning and then went up to the garden to pick the ripening vegetables and went back to my cabin as the sun was setting. As I climbed the steps to the porch, I noticed a shoe box sitting near my front door. I hurried to open it, and under crisp white tissue paper there was a pair of women's shoes in my size.

Even though I had witnessed this type of manifestation many times at the farm, I still couldn't quite believe it. The farm was a mile or so from a small town and it had only a gas station, a small grocery store and a post office. There was no note with the shoes and I assumed they came from the man who I saw that morning on the path. However, I had no idea where he came from, how he knew my shoe size and where he got them.

The next day I tried to find him so that I could thank him. When I asked a few of the people at the farm if they had seen him, I received blank stares. No one seemed to know who I was talking about. The next day, I asked a few others and still no one I spoke to had seen or heard of him. Although new people came to the farm, it was small enough that they were noticed. I never saw this man again and have come to believe that he might have been an angel.

When the first light snowfall of winter came, I had shoes. However, I still needed a new place to live. As much as I loved my cabin it had no insulation and no heat source. Reluctantly I moved into the only room available in the main house. It was small, dark and had an old squeaky single mattress. Every evening I heard a scratching sound coming from an outer wall. Initially I thought it was a branch from the tree outside. However, I checked and there were no tree branches touching the building or the windows. Still, every night I went to sleep to the sound of scratching. One night I noticed crumbling plaster at the base of the wall. As I watched more plaster flaked off little by little. Then the head of a rat peeped through and his rather large body followed. He too wanted in from the cold. A fierce-looking creature, I didn't want to share my room with him. Rats, I had learned, don't travel alone. If there was one, his family, cousins, and friends were not far behind. I was in no mood. After packing my things I went and slept on the couch that night. The next morning I asked within for direction as to where to go next.

Part V Spirits On Skid Row

Chapter 21

Thanksgiving with the Spirits

A homeless shelter in San Jose, California needed help and I was ready to go. My only problem was figuring out how I would get there as I didn't have enough money for a bus ticket. A well-traveled friend at the farm told me about an agency that hired people to drive cars to distant locations. I borrowed the farm's station wagon and made the two-hour trip to their office. When I learned there was a car that needed to be driven to San Jose as soon as possible, I knew it was meant to be.

The farm was a spiritual and magical place for me and it was not easy saying good-by. In addition to leaving the residents, volunteers and my cabin, I wondered if I was leaving Mary and St. Therese behind too. Maybe they belonged to the farm and those who lived and worked there.

On a gloomy cold day, I was dropped off at the car pick-up site with an abandoned dog that I decided to take with me. On my way into the building, I noticed an older-looking Ford Pinto parked out front. I laughed to myself wondering what it would be like to drive it across the country. After filling out more paperwork, I was given the keys and directed to the dull brown Ford Pinto that I had just laughed at.

A few hours into the drive I couldn't help but notice that every now and then people honked their horns and waved at me as they passed. I waved back, but didn't understand why I was getting so much attention. Later that day I walked behind the car at a rest stop and discovered the source of my popularity. A bright yellow bumper sticker that said, *Honk If You're A Sexy Senior Citizen.*

To save money and because I barely had any, I pulled into truck and rest stops to sleep. The car was uncomfortable and small, and I could only sleep two or three hours at a time. This allowed me to drive in the dark and quiet of the night when there were few cars on the road. Early Thanksgiving morning I drove through the flat farmland of the Midwest. Hungry and running out of gas I found an open gas station with a store attached to it. In an empty field I ate my tuna fish sandwich while my dog played. It was a chilly and windy but sunny day, and a few tears stung my eyes. I imagined my mother, my brothers and sister all together, and I wondered if they thought of me.

As I thought of what I was thankful for, whispers and gentle feelings of love and comfort began to creep ever so slowly into my heart. I was reminded of my younger days, crouched in the woods in the sunlight listening to my spirit friends. They had always been there for me, and in these moments of complete aloneness I was grateful that they were close.

Back on the road and about two-thirds of the way through the trip I started to feel fatigued. Sleeping in parking lots with a dog was not very restful. No matter what time of night it was, he felt it was his responsibility to let me know when a car or truck pulled in and out of the rest area.

One morning after driving several hours the night before and exhausted from lack of sleep, I encountered unexpected heavy traffic in the mountains in Colorado. I had been driving at a leisurely pace and suddenly it felt as if I had entered a race. Drivers were careening down the mountain highway on both sides of me and I started to feel anxious. With both hands gripped on the steering wheel I became increasing panicked. Instinctively I reached out to Mary for help. Almost immediately I felt her warm calming presence. I started to breathe again and was able to focus on the road. I even laughed at myself and found some humor in the situation. As much as I had resisted her presence, I was glad she was still with me.

The many miles and hours on the road induced a meditative state and intuitive insights flooded in. One surprising and persistent message I received was that I would meet my partner in San Jose. Traveling and living in different places did not give me much time to date and I wondered if I would ever meet someone.

Finally on a peaceful full moon starlit night, I drove through the California desert. The scent of sage filled the air and I relaxed. California felt welcoming, open and accepting, and I was glad that I had come back. After five days of driving and sleeping in the car, I made it to San Jose that afternoon.

The Catholic Worker was in an older part of the inner city, and after driving in circles, I eventually found it. A two-story brick building, it didn't look too different from the professional brick buildings on both sides of it. As I pulled into the driveway, I saw a dark-haired man about my age standing near the gate at the rear of the building. *So that's what he looks like*, I said to myself. Without a doubt I knew that this was the man that I had come to San Jose to meet. This intuitive knowing was as quick and clear as any other message that I had ever received. As I got out of my car, he walked toward me, glanced at the inside of my car and laughed.

"Your car's a mess," he said and walked away.

Chapter 22

The Other Side Gets Chatty

Although I had worked with a similar population in New York, nothing could have adequately prepared me for the San Jose house. The men's shelter and soup kitchen was a no frills and a bare bones environment. The three other volunteers had rooms in the upstairs of the two-story brick house and the downstairs rooms were filled with bunk beds and cots where homeless men spent the night. In the early evening a long line formed at the door and there was never enough room to accommodate all those in need. In the back of the property an addition had been built onto a garage and converted into a kitchen and dining room. This is where meals were cooked and served. In the morning and midday, men, women and children lined up for a meal. Most days the line extended around the corner and down the sidewalk. There was a sister house for women and children a short walk away that had a more settled and suburban atmosphere. However, it was the men's shelter and soup kitchen that needed help.

The first morning after my arrival I went and sat on the front steps. Across the street there was a vacant lot that homeless people frequented. On this particular morning there was a white van in the lot with several men huddled around it. When they noticed me whatever activity was going on halted and all eyes focused my way. A few minutes later a man crossed the street and sat down next to me. He was friendly but inquisitive. It was obvious that he had been sent to find out who I was and what I was doing there. After answering a few of his questions, I realized that I was interrupting something and probably needed to go back into the house, which I did. A few weeks later when I was better known and trusted, I asked one of the men what was happening that morning.

"Gun sale, just unloading some guns," he said and went back to eating his meal of beans and cornbread.

The needs of the homeless for shelter, food, clothing and compassion never ceased. From morning until night I was busy cooking, washing dishes or sheets, cleaning and meeting with the other volunteers and groups that came to help. Many of the homeless had addiction issues or mental or physical health problems. There were older people who had worked all their lives then fell on hard times and a few college students who couldn't afford housing. Some of those who lived under bridges and in the park had jobs, but didn't make enough to rent a home.

Day and night people showed up at the house when there was a drug overdose, health issue or if they needed a warm blanket or clothes. However, it was not just material needs that they came for. If they were sad, hungry, lonely or in need of comfort, they came, and unfortunately if they were angry or just wanted to complain, they also showed up. Most of the time I felt powerless to ease others' suffering in a significant way. Although I worked long hours day and night it didn't seem to make a dent.

As the needs of others consumed my available energy and attention, my reliance on the spirits intensified. No longer tentative and shy about asking for help, I turned to Mary and St. Therese for divine intervention. Not for my personal benefit, but as a force that could break through the difficulties and stress of those who most needed it. I wanted others to feel comforted and loved, and my ability to do this paled in comparison to what I knew they offered.

Spirits in the Hospital

Life on the streets was raw, lonely, noisy and quite often desperate. Yet there was a remarkable and at times miraculous spirit of community and giving among the homeless. The few belongings that they owned were either stuffed into a shopping cart and wheeled around day and night, or rolled up in a blanket or pillowcase and carried. Yet, if someone needed something that another had, it was freely shared or given. If there was one bottle of alcohol, it was passed around, as were cigarettes and food. On cold nights, it wasn't unusual for someone to give up their bed in the house to a less healthy and older man. For the most part there was an unexpected and inspirational caring and recognition of one another's suffering.

Many of the people who lived on the street suffered from ill health. One day, Bill, an older man who came to the house regularly for meals, collapsed and refused to go to the hospital by way of ambulance. After a little persuading he agreed to let some of the men get him into the home's truck and I drove him to the hospital. While sitting and waiting with him in the emergency room, I noticed a visibly upset well-dressed older couple. When the woman turned toward me, I smiled and said hello.

Staring down the hall, she said, "My granddaughter had a seizure this morning. My daughter called and told me to meet them here. No one will tell me anything, I think they are being seen. I am just so worried."

"I'm so sorry," I replied.

"Is that your grandfather?" she asked.

"He's a friend," I said.

She paused and looked at him slumped over his chair, and going in and out of consciousness. Unshaven and missing most of his teeth, his clothes were soiled and the smell of the streets and liquor clung to him. I don't know if his demeanor rattled her, but she turned and intently looked at me.

"Would you pray with me? We can pray right now," she said.

Although I was surprised by her request, I felt that this was the least I could do. I closed my eyes and asked Mary and St. Therese for healing and love for the little girl and for Bill. The woman prayed out loud, and as she did, I felt and saw a male spirit hovering close to Bill. The spirit told me that he was Bill's brother. I intuitively realized that Bill was sicker than I had thought and that he would soon be passing into the spirit realm.

When we finished praying the woman thanked me and a few minutes later her daughter came out of an examination room and sat with her.

When Bill's name was called, I woke him and tried to help him up. As I did I whispered in his ear that his brother was close and that his family loved him. He smiled and then hobbled off swaying to the left and right with the nurse. He never came back to the house, and a week or so later, I learned that he had passed over. I was thankful that his brother had come for him.

On the Way to the Funeral

Despite my focus on the practical needs of others, my awareness and connection with the spirit realm was intensifying. When people walked through the soup line or entered the house in the evening, I often saw spirits walking alongside them. Some of the spirits were aware of me but we didn't communicate or interact. However, a few were more vocal and persistent. One afternoon while riding the city bus, a larger man dressed in a suit got on and sat down beside me. Next to him was a woman spirit and I could feel how much she loved him.

He hung his head down, then said aloud.

"I'm going to my mother's funeral."

Although he looked down, I assumed he was talking to me.

"I'm sorry," I said.

"I don't want to miss it. I had car trouble. Of all days... can't believe this is happening."

As he talked the woman spirit standing next to him clutched her chest.

"Tell him, I love him. Please tell him," she said.

I was surprised by this request and tried to ignore her. However, she was not easily deterred.

"Please, tell him, I love him," she said again.

I knew that telling him this would give her peace. So, I turned to the man.

"Was your mom a larger woman with long dark hair that she wore in a bun on the top of her head?" I asked. He looked at me with tears in his eyes and said, "Yes, yes, that's her."

"Did she die suddenly of a heart attack?"

"Yes, she did. I feel so guilty. She called me the day before and I never called her back," he said. "How do you know this, tell me how?"

"She's with you and wants you to know that she loves you," I said.

More tears welled up in his eyes as he stared at me. Before he got a chance to say anything, I went to the front of the bus and got off at the next stop.

Chapter 23

Encounter with Evil

Despite the suffering and hardship, the presence of a divine and loving power was evident in the small acts of kindness and sense of community among the homeless. However, fear, violence, loneliness and negativity were always present, ready to claim the vulnerable. There were many defenseless and tenderhearted people who lived on the streets and quite often it was this naivety that had caused them to lose everything. Many had been financially or emotionally taken advantage of, trusted the wrong people or they were just not able to figure out and deal with the high demands of daily life. As homeless wanderers they were easy victims for angry, confused and mentally ill people who didn't care or notice who they bullied.

Along with full moons, cold nights were some of the most dangerous times for the vulnerable homeless. Men who didn't normally frequent the shelter came seeking a warm bed and escape from the weather. Usually these men stayed away from the shelters as they were more loners who had difficulties in getting along with others. They didn't enjoy the close quarters, and sleeping next to others was a challenge.

One evening during a long cold spell, the men lined up in front of the house eager to come in. As I made the beds and put out toiletries before opening the door, something felt off to me. When I looked out the window at the men shivering in the cold, I started to feel anxious. It felt as if something was up and it wasn't good. Although there was no reason to go outside, I put on my coat and went out the front door. Before I made it to the bottom of the front steps, I saw a man who I didn't recognize push his body against a smaller man. When he stepped back, I saw blood on his coat and a knife in his hand. On the ground with blood spilling from his stomach was James, a frequent guest at the shelter. A quiet man in his fifties, James at one time had a home, job and family. One of his children, a boy, had a heart condition and after their insurance ran out, James struggled to keep up with the medical expenses. After his son died during surgery, James became depressed and despondent and lost his job. A year or so later his wife left him and he drifted to the streets. James was not one to cause problems, he was kind to others and stayed away from trouble.

A couple of the men in line helped me to put pressure on his wounds and one of the volunteers called an ambulance. Soon after they left with James, the police arrived. A few hours later they arrested the man suspected of stabbing him.

No one on the street knew why this happened. Oscar, the young man arrested for the stabbing, was a drifter. He showed up looking for shelter and was agitated that he had to wait in line in the cold. James, it seemed, was in the wrong place at the wrong time. Fortunately there was no internal damage and James was released to the care of his sister about a week later.

Not too long after this incident a few of the volunteers asked me if I wanted to go to the jail to visit the men from the street who were incarcerated. This was a common practice at the Catholic Worker where the gospels were taken seriously. In the book of Matthew in the Bible it says,

For I was hungry and you gave me something to eat, I was thirsty and you gave me something to drink, I was a stranger and you invited me in, I needed clothes and you clothed me, I was sick and you looked after me, I was in prison and you came to visit me.

For some reason, I felt compelled to meet with Oscar and this confused me. As I was not feeling particularly compassionate or forgiving toward him.

After a short wait, Oscar and I sat looking at each other

between a dirty smeared plexiglass partition. He was younger than I thought, likely in his early twenties. A thin man with dark hair and random beard stubble, he seemed happy to see me. When I told him that I worked at the shelter where he was arrested, he just smiled. I talked a little bit about the man that he stabbed and how he was going to be all right. Still he smiled and I realized that he may have thought that I was impressed with his violence. There was no sense of remorse or guilt in his words or expression.

When I looked into his eyes and intuitively felt his energy, a chill ran up my spine. A heavy and disturbing presence seemed to surround him. There was a darkness within him that I had never encountered and I intuitively realized that this was evil. I knew that as much as he was smiling and happy to see me, he could just as well hurt me and still smile. Although I had encountered and had to contend with dangerous and sociopathic people on the streets, this felt different. It was not until I looked into Oscar's eyes that I believed in evil.

A week or so after our visit, Oscar's court-appointed attorney called me and asked for my impression of Oscar and his crime. I was honest and told him that I believed Oscar to be dangerous and he would likely hurt others for no reason or purpose.

"Prison may be the best place for him," I said.

If he was looking for a character witness in his defense he didn't find it in me.

When I asked my guides about Oscar and the heavy darkness I felt in his presence they told me that there are lower entities with evil intent that hover close to the earth. However, they cannot simply take over someone's body or consciousness or make choices for another. Instead when our consciousness is weakened through alcohol or drug abuse, physical, emotional or mental abuse, or when we know we can benefit from another's misfortune and seek to take advantage of them, we invite them in.

"Is it possible to help someone if they have dark attachments?" I asked.

"We wanted you to become more aware of this kind of possession," I heard. "For now, practice compassion and pray for Oscar and the man he attacked. They both need intervention and healing. In the future you will learn how to release others from these attachments."

"Oh great, can't wait to take on this kind of evil," I thought.

Chapter 24

Meeting the Guru

When I first arrived in San Jose, there was one other woman working at the men's shelter. Juanita had come with her boyfriend from New York to volunteer. In their mid-thirties they were Puerto Rican and impressed me with being both street smart and spiritually sophisticated. They had been at the house in San Jose a little over a year and were making plans to return to the Bronx. Both of them were devotees of Baba Muktananda, an Indian teacher and guru, who had an ashram in Oakland, not too far from San Jose. The weekend before they were to leave, Juanita invited me to go with her to the ashram for a special celebration. Muktananda had been traveling for almost a year and he was returning to Oakland.

Ever since I read *The Autobiography of a Yogi* by Paramahansa Yogananda while in high school, I wanted to meet a guru. On my first trip to California, I went to Yoganada's Self-Realization Fellowship Center in Encinitas, California. Although I felt his great love and presence while staring out into the ocean from the cliffs on his property, I wanted to be in the physical presence of an enlightened master.

We arrived at the ashram at dusk to a festive and colorful party-like atmosphere with people streaming in and out of the center. Many wearing flowing saris seemed to drift along in a cloud of sweet-smelling patchouli incense. We squeezed our way in and sat on the floor shoulder to shoulder with enthusiastic devotees. The mood was infectious and I joined in and swayed, chanted and absorbed the electricity and heightened sense of expectancy that filled the room. Periodically someone announced that Baba was on his way, but arriving later than expected. This didn't seem to bother anyone. The chanting became louder and sweat poured down my back as I tried to keep up with the rhythmic swaying. Late into the night we learned that Baba had arrived and the fevered chanting and heightened anticipation became more intense. Some stood and recited unintelligible monologues while waving their hands in the air like the wings of fluttering birds. A few then collapsed into the arms of attendants who stood to catch them.

As Baba made his way to his seat in the front of the crowd, the energy of the room reached an almost fevered pitch. A thin middle-aged man dressed in a simple sari, the smile in his eyes lit up the room. He sat in front of us surrounded by attendants who directed us row by row to stand and silently take our turn kneeling in front of him to receive shaktipat. An energy transfusion of enlightenment from a holy person, Baba's touch or shaktipat was legendary. Juanita told me stories of people who were instantly awakened, healed and enlightened, or had spontaneous openings of their third eye and saw visions during these ceremonies.

As I stood in line, I watched as those before me received shaktipat and dreamily fell back in bliss or walked away swooning, some with tears in their eyes. When it came my turn to kneel down at Muktananda's feet, he lightly touched my forehead with his peacock feather. For a moment I felt the powerful transmission of his dynamic energy and love. When I lifted my head and looked up into his eyes I wanted to feel bliss and be transported to a higher spiritual awareness. Instead, I was shaken out of the experience by something that felt off and not right. Instead of love and an expansion of consciousness, I felt unsettled, cautious and alert. As I walked outside into the cool air, I was confused as to what had just happened.

It took me a few days to realize that what I felt in Muktananda's presence was the creepy feeling that warned me away from others. However, this made no sense. He was obviously loved and a master teacher and guru with ashrams and centers all over the world. Yet, I couldn't shake the feeling that there was something besides holiness and love that I felt in his presence. Several years later, I came across an article accusing him of physical and sexual abuse. Some of his females devotees had come forward after his death with the accusations. This saddened me, but it felt true.

Chapter 25

More Than Spiritual Love

Despite their hardships and suffering, most of the people who frequented the soup kitchen were caring and enjoyable to be with. Jerri was a few years older than me and an artist. He lived in a small apartment not far from the Worker and had a job. However, he often ate at the kitchen and drank with his friends who lived on the street. Everyone seemed to like Jerri. He was funny and generous, and despite his street smarts, he had an unassuming innocence. We became friends and took walks where he would point out the different architecture and art in the city.

During the time that Jerri and I became close, I was often alone at night in the house. There were only two other volunteers and they were both political activists who went to meetings and get-togethers several nights a week. Being alone in the large house with men who had mental health, alcohol and other issues was not something I enjoyed.

I wasn't in love with Jerri, but I sure did like his company. The men liked him and he had an easygoing and calming effect on others. He often spent the night at the house with me which helped me to feel safer. However, this did not go over well with the community of volunteers. In one of our weekly meetings a volunteer from the women's house voiced her disapproval of our relationship and his being allowed to stay the night. Others chimed in, and when it was brought to a vote, he was out.

During the meeting I chain-smoked and felt picked on. There seemed to be a fine line between us and them, and I wasn't sure where I landed. The group in San Jose did not have the same open and accepting nature as the farm. There were a few devout Catholics and political activists who more easily separated themselves from the homeless and those that frequented the soup kitchen. It wasn't so easy for me.

Although I was a volunteer and did not suffer from an addiction or mental health issue, I was very close to being homeless and had been for a while. With no money or marketable job skills, there was little that differentiated me from those who looked to the Worker for help. The stark truth was that I had nothing. Being psychic and talking to dead people didn't feel like a viable career option and yet this was all I had. Although it provided me with emotional and spiritual sustenance I didn't consider it money in the bank. Exhausted by the continuous demands of the homeless and the judgments of some of the volunteers, I felt increasingly isolated. I imagined myself to be God's string puppet, twisting and turning with no sense of where I was going and if I was up for the task.

The Fulfillment

I continued to take walks with Jerri, but he came to the house less and less, and eventually faded out of my life. Around this time, Daniel, the man who I met when I first arrived at the San Jose house, started to frequent the house more often. An ex-Benedictine monk, he lived a few blocks away in a house with three ex-nuns and worked as a handyman at the local Catholic church. Before being a monk, he had studied to be a priest. However, it was hard to believe that he sat in quiet contemplation in a monastery for five years or took on vows of the religious life. Outgoing and irreverent, Daniel didn't take much seriously. While most of the community in San Jose tended to be more solemn about their convictions, he bounced around and either made others laugh or irritated them.

After Daniel and his girlfriend broke up he began to spend more time at the house. He was funny and easy to be with him and we became friends. While walking through the city one afternoon, we went into a store that sold sports-related items.

As soon as we went in I noticed a rack of bathing suits. These were not lay in the sun or wade in the ocean bikinis, they were suits for more serious lap swimming. When I was younger I was a competitive swimmer, but had not swum in years.

Daniel must have seen me longingly looking at the suits and offered to buy me one. I was stunned. These suits were not cheap, and although he worked at the church, it was just part-time. His afternoons were often spent watching cartoons. I couldn't resist this offer, and with bathing suit in hand, I walked out of the store feeling lighter and happier.

There was a university pool not too far from the house and a friend of the community was able to get me a pool pass. Although a couple of members of the community thought that swimming was a luxury that took me away from the house unnecessarily, there was nothing that could stop me. Swimming laps was meditative and gave me the quiet contemplation time that I desperately needed. Daniel's offer to buy me a bathing suit changed my life in other ways as well.

While I opened my heart to those in need, allowing another to be there for me was another matter altogether. I have heard it said that one act of kindness can change a person's life and this is what happened to me. I began to trust Daniel in a way that I had not previously been able to. Little by little I shared more about myself, including my psychic inclinations. Despite his devotion to Catholicism and more traditional religion, he didn't seem too taken aback by my experiences, but I didn't push it either. I didn't want to focus on and overwhelm him or anyone with my psychic self. I was just enough concerned about what others thought and their judgments that I didn't overshare. However, I'm not sure all of this would have mattered. We recognized a kindred spirit within one another and our connection was fun and adventurous. One night a couple of months into our friendship, there was a knock on my bedroom door. Daniel came in and climbed the ladder up to my platform bed.

A few months later, an ex-nun friend of Daniel's asked him if we would be interested in going to Mexico to build water systems in remote indigenous villages. The reply was a resounding yes, and within a few weeks we were on a bus to San Cristobal de las Casas in Chiapas, Mexico.

Part VI Spirits of Another Land

Chapter 26

Mayan Spirits

Having worked in the inner city of San Jose among the poor and destitute, I didn't expect to be shocked by the poverty of Mexico, but I was. Immediately after crossing the border into Tijuana, row after row of large cardboard boxes that housed the poor spread out like an out of control field of dandelions. Not too far away the wealthy shops and homes of Southern California stood in stark contrast.

As we slowly drove through the streets, children wearing torn and dirty clothes ran up to the car windows. Holding up small packets of gum and candy, they yelled, "*Chiclets, chiclets,*" in the hope of making a sale. The elderly, ill and drunk sat against their shelters or on the side of the streets staring into the sun or watching the cars as they whizzed by. The noise of the city was loud and constant. Honking horns, drivers yelling at one another, music from small shops, laughter, arguing and the squeals of children playing all blended together into a steady hum. There was constant activity, and despite the overwhelming heat, people were out and about. The scent of roasted meat, grilled corn tortillas, liquor, and car and bus fumes drifted into a cloud that hung heavy in the air.

Daniel's mother lived close to the Mexican border and drove us to the bus station. She went to Tijuana often and knew her way around. After a long hot wait in a large parking lot that was the bus station, we made our way onto the bus. An extension of the activity, sounds and smells of the streets, most of the passengers carried their things in large cloth bundles and bags that they stuffed under their seats. Loud music played over the bus speakers and the smell of grilled meat and tortillas floated down the aisle.

For the next several days the bus took us into the open desert and through large and small towns. Sometimes we exited the highway and drove for miles on sandy roads only to stop in front of a Coca-Cola sign in the desert where a few people would get off and on.

When we arrived in Mexico City we entered a maze of confusion and I realized that my high school Spanish class didn't do much to enable me to converse. Our bus ticket only took us this far and we were on our own to figure out how to complete our journey to the southernmost part of Mexico. After consulting my Spanish/English dictionary I was able to ask a few questions, but completely unable to understand the answers I received. Most assumed that Daniel was Mexican and rattled off information to him at a breakneck speed. I was lucky if I caught one or two words. Daniel's grandparents had emigrated to California from Mexico and his mother was fluent in Spanish. However, she wanted him to be an American, and except for a few curse words and other expressions, he was not encouraged to speak Spanish.

In San Cristobal de las Casas

Eventually we made our way by taxi to the other side of town and got on another bus. This one was filled with a slightly different population. We were headed into the rural and indigenous areas of Mexico and many of the passengers wore more traditional woven clothing and carried machetes and handmade leather and woven bags. After many hours and miles of staring out the window at the flat and dusty landscape, the bus started to climb. As we wound around rich and lush green mountainous terrain we were treated to spectacular views. The highway deteriorated into a mostly bumpy road with no dividing line. Traffic was sparse and every so often we passed a truck with a full bed of animals or men wearing straw hats. Eventually we made our way into a colonial-looking town, and the bus stopped and opened its doors at the zócalo or center. This was our destination, San Cristobal de las Casas in Chiapas, and it was unlike any other town that we had passed through on our bus trip through Mexico. There were no paved roads or modern-looking buildings, only a few cars and it felt reminiscent of another era. This was in the late 70s, before the Internet, cable TV or cell phones, and outside influences were minimal.

The main hub of trade for the many different groups of indigenous people who lived in the surrounding area, San Cristobal had a rich history of resistance to outside invaders and contemporary influences. When the Spanish arrived in the 16th century, they battled the local Native Mexicans for control of the area. After years of fighting without much progress, the Spanish moved on to more lucrative areas of Mexico. Because of the rugged mountain area, the lack of mineral wealth and little access to markets, the area was more or less left alone. It lived in relative peace as an independent state, until 1822 when the Mexican government declared Chiapas a state. After many years of liberal and conservative governmental fighting and arguing about what to do with the area, the government powers that be too moved on and Chiapas once again became one of the largest indigenous populations in the country.

As we made our way through the center of town, barefoot Native Mexicans with large bags of handmade goods and vegetables loaded onto their backs and strapped to their foreheads moved up and down the streets at a swift pace. Although we had the address of the house that the volunteer organization provided, there were few street names and numbers to guide us. After being pointed in the right direction by an eager-to-help man, we stood before thick adobe and plaster walls and knocked on a tall wooden gate. A smiling older woman wearing an apron greeted us in Spanish and introduced herself as Maria, our *cocinero* or cook.

Despite the noise of the street, it was quiet and peaceful

inside the walls. The older and more colonial main part of the house had thick adobe walls that kept it dark and cool even in the summer heat. There was a newer section added onto the house where we stayed. Between the older and newer sections was a large garden of flowers and vegetables. Although we had plumbing, the toilet and shower shared space. When taking a shower the toilet would fill with water, often overflowing. There was no heat or air conditioning in the house and only part of it had electricity. Fortunately, unlike the intense heat of most of Mexico, the highlands of Chiapas had a more moderate climate.

Another volunteer about our age from the Midwest arrived a week or so after we did. He was a strong-looking guy and easygoing. Maria our cook also lived with her teenage son on the property. Initially I felt uncomfortable having a cook, but I soon came to understand how much she valued her position. The organization we volunteered with was called Grupo Creo, or I Believe. It began as a group of doctors who went into the indigenous villages to help heal and tend to the ill. Several years into the project it became clear that most of the illnesses being treated were the result of contaminated water. There were no plumbing or outhouses in the villages and the Native Mexicans collected their water from the streams and rivers. Over time the emphasis of the project changed from medical care to building simple gravity-fed water systems to provide the community with clean water.

As anxious as we were to get started, we arrived during the rainy season. A subtropical climate, when it rained, it rained hard. Getting to the villages was nearly impossible and constructing a water system was out of the question. The free time gave us the opportunity to attend a language school.

Every morning for a few weeks we went to an older open air building in the center of town and talked to a personal tutor. Mine was an attractive young woman with long black hair. Even though it was a casual atmosphere, she showed up every day looking like a runway model. She wore stylish dresses and heels, every hair was in place and her makeup was flawless. In turn I wore my usual, jeans, tee shirt and sandals. My tutor was all business, and as I practiced conversing with her in Spanish we were often interrupted by bursts of laughter coming from the other side of an adobe wall that separated us from Daniel and his tutor. Daniel's version of language school included teaching his tutor how to swear and say funny things in English and learning the same in Spanish.

There were no phones or mail in the indigenous areas of the highlands. As the rains lessened all we could do was wait for the Native Mexicans to come to us when they were ready. In the meantime we did a lot of walking. San Cristobal de las Casas had many churches which were open all day, every day. There were also many missions and missionaries in the area. The Mormons, Baptists, Christians, Methodists, and others were there to save pagan souls and teach the Native Mexicans about God. However, like all of Mexico, the area was predominantly Catholic, and above all other saints and divine beings, Guadalupe was the most revered and honored. The larger churches had elaborate shrines with brightly-painted statues of her lit with candles and incense. Simple handmade altars to Guadalupe could also be found in alleys and along the roadside. Because the area was made up of different groups of Native Mexicans all who had deep roots in earth-based spirituality, the churches embraced both Mayan and Catholic traditions. Along with Guadalupe most of them had at least one full-sized skeleton encased in a glass casket. These often wore crowns made of crystals and stones, and were draped in hand-woven shawls with the colors and patterns of the different tribes.

One afternoon we encountered a parade and celebration outside of a church. Dancers in colorful costumes that depicted saints, birds and animals wound up and down the street to the beat of drums and wooden flutes. Usually quiet and reserved, the Native Mexicans, many in full headdresses and masks, danced with abandon and devotion.

Standing in the sunlight watching the colorful festive event, I noticed a male dancer wearing a mask that resembled an eagle flying through the air. Tossing his head up into the sky he let out a birdlike call and then spun around and around in a circle. As he did this a gold glowing orb of light shot out of his chest and flew above his head. The orb appeared to dance along with him, moving and swirling in the air. Fascinated by this unexpected show of energy and light, I watched as other costumed and trance-like dancers paraded down the street. They too cast light and colorful orbs of energy into the sky.

Not accustomed to this kind of vibrant display of energy, I watched in fascination. As the Native Mexicans celebrated the spirits through song, dance and prayer, the boundaries between the physical and spiritual blurred. Soaking in the dancers' electrifying intensity, I felt a part of the native people's ancestral web of life, both physical and nonphysical.

My Teacher

A week or so later I passed a small storefront that had beautiful and intricate hand-woven rugs and clothing hanging in the window and felt an intuitive nudge to go in. An art collective that exhibited and sold high quality crafts made by skilled Native Mexican craftspeople, they also offered private lessons. I couldn't pass this up and the next afternoon I sat on a stone floor in a small quiet open courtyard and began my first lesson. My teacher, an older Native Mexican woman with a long greying black braid, did not speak much Spanish and taught mostly through example and gestures.

The traditional looms were made with sticks and fiber. One end wrapped around the waist and the other end was tied to a tree or whatever was handy. This created the tension needed to weave. With rapt attention, I watched as my teacher tied one end of the loom to a pole, sat down and turned a clump of string and spun wool into cloth. When it was my turn to try I was all thumbs. The strings didn't move in place like they did for my teacher. After several attempts on my own, she moved closer and through patient gestures we were able to set up the loom. In between classes I practiced for hours and eventually began to get the hang of it.

As the classes progressed, I began to establish a better rapport with my teacher. She spoke to me in her language and I taught her a little English. When speaking in her native tongue, her mood lightened and she laughed at my mistakes and awkwardness. Eventually I found myself lulled into a meditative state as I pulled the yarn back and forth. This simple kind of loom had been used for centuries, and as my teacher watched me weave, I felt as if I was traveling back through time and finding my place within the great web of feminine energy. The patterns she taught me to create contained symbolic images of corn, the sky and the earth, and had likely been similar to those woven by her Mayan ancestors.

We met for several weeks, and toward the end of our series of classes, she appeared to me in a dream one night. At first I wasn't certain that it was her. In a misty kind of vision, I saw an older woman with a long braid smiling and then the dream ended. This happened a couple of times; then one night I saw her more clearly. In this dream that felt more like a spirit visitation, she laughed and then turned and walked into the jungle. I followed and tried to keep up with her as she wove in and out of the thick vegetation. Loud birds called in the distance and I felt a humid damp warmth on my skin. I woke up feeling disoriented and restless. A few nights later, she appeared to me again and led me through the dark jungle to a sparkling fast-moving river. On the other side of the river there were indigenous-looking people waving and trying to get my attention. They seemed to be welcoming me and I realized that I had dark skin and a short, strong body just like them. I felt powerful, seen and known. My teacher sent me a message to sit down by a fire that was suddenly in front of me. The sky was dark, and as I looked up, the stars seemed to be talking and laughing. It felt as if all of life knew me and wanted to communicate. Everything was alive and I felt at peace.

I woke up the next morning sad that it had only been a dream. A couple of days later in class my teacher watched me weave then looked in my eyes and said, "Estas listas." *You are done.*

Chapter 27

The Indigenous Saints

Once the rains ended we began to get requests to go into villages to determine if it was possible to install water systems. I was eager to get started but a little intimidated when it came to the work itself. Before coming to Mexico, we attended a few meetings with a former volunteer who went over a few basics, but mostly talked about his experiences and shared memories. Although I thought I had a general idea of what we were going to do, the reality of the work was becoming more clear. The two other volunteers were confident in their mechanical abilities, I was not. My hands-on work experience was limited to painting and changing light bulbs.

Getting to the villages also proved to be an unexpected challenge. Only a few buses went into the more remote regions in the mountains. Instead men in pickup trucks drove the main roads looking for passengers, and for a small fee people, animals and equipment rode in the truck bed.

The first village we visited involved a full day of travel and fortunately we were able to find a bus that took us most of the way. Filled with Native Mexicans taking whatever they hadn't been able to sell in town back to their village, most were carrying large cloth bags of woven clothing, food and wood for fires or chickens.

After a long half-day of going up and down mountains in an old school bus, we stopped and the driver pointed to the door, signaling our stop. As we stepped off of the bus, several men and a donkey came out of the bush to take us the rest of the way by foot. The path that led to the village was busy with Native Mexicans carrying bundles on their backs and strapped to their foreheads. Some of the women also had a baby wrapped in a shawl on their chest, and despite the heavy loads, they ran at a steady pace. With the heat and intense humidity of the area, it was all I could do to keep up with the others. After several hours of hiking we arrived at the village. I was exhausted and sat on a wood stump near a fast-flowing river where several women were busy washing clothes. Children played close by splashing water and chasing one another. Up the hill from where I sat there were large gardens and mud and straw adobe huts with thatched twig roofs and dirt floors.

Daniel who had gone off with one of the men called to me to join him in a tour of the village. After winding through an intricate system of gardens, we stopped at the cement block one-room schoolhouse. A source of pride for the village, it had been built to meet government requirements. This basically meant that it was cinderblock and not adobe mud and straw. Off to the side of the school was a small adobe hut with a door made with sticks that resembled jail bars. After a little back and forth interpretation, I learned that in order to have a teacher come in from town, the village had to have a jail. When I asked if anyone had ever spent time in it, I was given a curious look, but no answer. I thought maybe I didn't ask the question correctly and tried again. This time the young man opened the jail door and got in. Smiling from behind the stick jail bars, he said, "Si, esta carcel es buena," or *Yes, this jail is good.*

Hungry from our hike, we then sat down to a meal of beans and the best corn tortillas I have ever eaten. Afterward the men went to a separate area to talk. I was invited to join some of the women in an adjacent hut. Most of the women spoke their tribe's language and a few talked to me in Spanish. As I sat on the mud floor and watched them weave, and nurse their babies, I felt an ease and tranquility that I hadn't felt in a long time. After witnessing the suffering and the loneliness of the inner-city poor and homeless, life in the highlands of Chiapas felt like an oasis.

After a restful night on a cot in the school room, we rose

at dawn to hike to the ojo de agua or eye of the water. This is where the underground spring that supplied the cleanest water surfaced. Because the system was gravity-fed, it had to be well above the village.

Being a tall white woman with curly red hair, I didn't blend in. As we made our way through the village some of the Native Mexicans stopped in their tracks and stared at me. Wide-eyed children hid behind their mothers and only the very brave initially came close. However, this shyness was usually short-lived. As they became more comfortable with me, the children followed close behind.

As I observed the villagers throughout the coming days, they reminded me of a school of fish or flock of birds. They seemed to move in natural unison with one another and with the heavens and spirit realm. Ancient indigenous tradition guided their daily rituals and united the community with the earth and skies. Their Mayan ancestors hovered close to the villagers as they worked and danced. They sat among them as they ate, and came to life on the altars.

Immersed in a community that recognized and honored spirits, I became aware of how much was lacking in our more modern societal spiritual beliefs. With no acknowledgment of our loved ones in spirit, we all too often feel adrift and alone in the vast expanse of the unseen realm, unable to receive our ancestors' gifts of love, wisdom and guidance.

On my last evening in the village I was invited into the women's hut. As I watched them work, laugh and gossip, I gazed out the open doorway and noticed a shrine in the distance. It was a simple stone altar with a wooden painted image of what appeared to be Guadalupe propped up against it. There were a few wildflowers in clay containers surrounding it.

One of the women noticed my interest and pointed to the altar and asked me in Spanish if I liked it.

I told her I did and asked her if this was for Guadalupe.

"Si, si," she said.

I said something about Guadalupe being powerful and her eyes grew wide.

"Si ella es poderosa y fuerte," she said. *Yes, she is powerful and strong.*

As she spoke our eyes met and I think we both recognized Guadalupe as a common ally and unifying spirit.

A Lesson in Authenticity

Although images of Guadalupe were common in the villages, she was not worshipped as the Catholic icon of the modern church. Instead she embodied the earth-based divine feminine and represented the indigenous orientation. As the personification of the earthly cycles of birth, death and renewal, Guadalupe was the kind of goddess that the Native Mexicans could identify with. With a desire to save souls through religious indoctrination, missionaries likely did not expect this kind of adaptability. The Maya people cleverly managed to weave together the spirits and their gods and goddesses with the Church's holy saints. Like highly trained and skilled negotiators, they incorporated religious attitudes and beliefs, and found a place at the table with the Christian, Catholic and Mormon missions that had infiltrated the area.

The Native Mexicans' ability to accept and blend with the non-indigenous lifestyle cropped up in other ways as well. There were many different and distinct groups of Native Mexicans in Chiapas, and some lived so deep in the bush they were rarely seen. One such group was distinctive in their look and demeanor. Unlike most of the other Native Mexicans who wore colorful clothing and regularly interacted with the Mexicans who lived in town, this group wore plain beige woven tunics and didn't cut or brush their hair. Every now and then, I caught a glimpse of a small group in the jungle or on a bus.

However, despite their austere and primitive lifestyle, many wore gold watches. This was interesting as it didn't seem as if they had any use for them. Time in the jungle was not measured by our standard methods. There were no clocks and watches in the villages. When setting up meetings with the Native Mexicans, we only specified morning, afternoon or evening. Yet, despite the vague illusiveness of time, we never had to wait for anyone. As soon as we got off a bus or met in town, someone from the village would be there to meet us. Similarly if we were out in the bush and had to get to a bus or truck at a certain time, the Native Mexicans would somehow know when to leave.

The gold watch Native Mexicans were land rich. A valuable and rare type of tree had been discovered on their property and they allowed some of the wood to be harvested and sold. Perhaps they simply liked the look of the watches or their tree business required them to regulate their time by conventional standards. Whatever the motivation, they wore them along with their simple beige woven tunics and a machete strapped to their back.

It was this kind of adaptability that allowed the Maya people to survive and retain their authentic roots. Through their humility and simplicity, they graciously accepted what was offered, be it religion, money, watches or water systems, and found a place for it in their culture. Yet despite their yielding and constant accommodation to outsiders, the Native Mexicans had a well-earned skepticism when it came to trusting non-indigenous people. Although they adapted to the beliefs and practices of the predominant culture, they knew that their level of understanding and acceptance would not be reciprocated. They didn't discuss and promote their spirituality and they certainly didn't argue with the missionaries that persistently preached the way to salvation. They smiled, nodded their heads and went about their business. It was only through observation and the occasional remark or explanation that they revealed their true beliefs.

More often they offered their wisdom though their actions, and their kind and peaceful demeanor. Their ability to both resist and flow with the ever-changing outer world while retaining and preserving their culture was an important and timely lesson for me. As shape shifters they moved in and out of the seemingly opposing worlds with their authenticity intact. It was this ability to blend together their traditional spirituality and way of life with the modern world that was constantly and consistently encroaching on their land and beliefs that helped me to confront my own crisis of identity.

Through the different places I had traveled to and the people I encountered, I had searched for a reflection of myself in the world. I wanted something outside of me, a group or belief system that matched my inner self and provided a sense of identity. In Chiapas I realized that I didn't need to fit in and be understood. I could accept truth as it flowed into my life and it didn't need to be fully reconciled with every other truth. It only had to make sense to me. I could be a contradiction. However others defined being psychic and communicating with the other side did not have to be my concern. For all of the misunderstanding that I had experienced and was yet to experience, I only had to be me and be aware of the clear chord of truth that resounded in my heart. I knew who I was and it was okay if I couldn't find anything or anyone in the outer world that matched my sense of self. My self-worth was not dependent on being like others or being understood.

Chapter 28

Marriage in the Ruins of Palenque

Although I was surrounded by indigenous people who honored, revered and consulted the spirits on such matters as to where to plant a garden and how to heal an earache or a foul mood, I was surprisingly more grounded than I had ever been. Spending time with Daniel also helped me to integrate the two worlds I had always been balancing. He had an outgoing and extroverted personality, and I often wondered how he had been able to be a monk. His constant jokes, warmth and laughter slowly allowed me to accept the love and connection that those in the physical realm had to offer.

When not out in the bush, Daniel and I explored the area. One of our favorite pastimes was climbing the long steep stairs up to the Guadalupe Church. Situated high on a hill it offered a panoramic view of the city and distant mountains. Afterward we often went to a cafe for fresh fruit juice or a strong coffee. Two young indigenous men also frequented the cafe and we became friends. Although they were Native Mexican, they didn't wear traditional woven clothing. Instead they wore slacks and button-down shirts, and seemed to be trying to assimilate into the modern Mexican culture. Although language was a bit of a barrier we all bopped our heads while the jukebox played Donna Summer's disco hit *Hot Stuff* over and over.

As Daniel and I grew closer our relationship deepened and we discussed our future. The ingenious and Mexican culture opened new possibilities for me. Centered in the here and now, I was among people who lived close to the earth, had babies, sold their vegetables and crafts, and honored and listened to the spirits and their ancestors. I wanted this and Daniel did too. Although I was in no position to contemplate having a child, this didn't stop me.

One day I casually said to Daniel, "I want to have a baby."

A few moments of silence followed. Then he said, "Okay, but I want to be married if I have a child."

A few more moments of silence followed and I said, "Okay."

Pretty easy. While it might have taken other couples years to discuss and make these decisions, we hammered it out in under three minutes. With two of the biggest decisions in our lives decided, we had to figure out the next steps. Although we were not in a rush to get married, our time frame accelerated when Daniel's mother decided to come for a visit.

When Daniel mentioned to his mother that we were thinking of getting married, she immediately pounced into action and said that she would be there as soon as she could. Daniel's grandparents came to the United States from Mexico. However, they considered themselves Spanish, not Mexican. Their ancestors were from the Basque region of Spain and this was an important distinction for them. Daniel's mother's first language was Spanish and she looked forward to driving through Mexico in her Cadillac with her third husband. Tradition was important to his family, and it was expected and assumed that we would get married in the Catholic Church. Daniel's mother wanted us to have a large wedding with all of his extended family in attendance. However, we wanted to get married in Mexico in a simple wedding. Although she accepted our decision, she never budged on her expectation that we marry in the Catholic Church.

Although I didn't want to disappoint her, I knew exactly where I wanted to get married and it wasn't the Church. The Mayan ruins of Palenque were a short bus ride away and my heart was set on getting married there.

Since my arrival in Chiapas I had become fascinated with the Mayan ruins and had studied and learned as much as I could about them. The ancient Mayans developed one of the most sophisticated cultures in the Western Hemisphere. Along with their accurate and complex calendar, they developed an intricate system of astronomy, astrology and built elaborate pyramids and temples. At the height of their civilization, which began in 250 CE, they had forty cities, each with a population somewhere between 5,000 to 50,000. Sometime around 900 BCE their cities collapsed, for reasons that are still unknown. At that time the social structure of the Mayan Empire became fragmented and the Mayans dispersed into smaller units throughout Southern Mexico and Northern Central America.

A once important and majestic Mayan city, Palenque flourished in the 7th century. In its day it was one of the largest spiritual, cultural and economic meccas of the Mayans. Surrounded by dense jungle, archaeologists estimated that only 5% of Palenque had been uncovered. The unearthed structures included several pyramids and temples accessed by tall steep steps and the palace which was a series of several buildings and courtyards. Near the ball court was a nine-story tower and the remnants of an advanced aqueduct system. Most of the structures were decorated with elaborately-carved reliefs. These intricate stone carvings explained the rites, daily life, practices and rituals of the Mayans, and honored many of the revered leaders who were encased deep under the pyramids.

As excited as I was about getting married in Palenque, Daniel was concerned that his mother would not necessarily understand or enjoy watching her son say his *I do's* on a pyramid. So we decided to go to Palenque before she arrived. This was not the best way to get on the good side of my future mother-in-law and she never let me forget it.

With a few things thrown into a backpack, we boarded a second-class bus that looked as if it would not make it across town. As rickety as it appeared to be, no one else seemed concerned. Mariachi music blared from a cassette player as the bus slowly climbed and then descended zigzag down the hills. When the bus teetered too close to the edge of a cliff the brakes screeched and we swerved back over to the other side of the dirt road. Unfazed by the harrowing drive, the other passengers, all Native Mexicans, tightly held onto their bundles and looked straight ahead.

When we got off the bus in Palenque the heat and humidity was stifling. We were no longer in the mountains and the air was heavy and sticky. It was just before sunset and we had less than thirty minutes before the park closed.

Our plan was to quickly survey the ruins and find a spot for our wedding early the next morning. However, the expansive pyramids and other structures made focusing difficult. I became disoriented by the sheer energetic force of the uncovered civilization. Spirits roamed freely and their powerful energy was continually being broadcast. I asked my guides to lead me to the perfect place and Daniel followed looking as overwhelmed as I felt. When we came to an area of thicker jungle vegetation with a few smaller structures, I knew this was the spot. Before we got a chance to take a further look, a park ranger yelled to us that the park was closing and the buses would soon be leaving.

The Temple of the Rising Sun

After a warm and noisy night at a rundown hotel in the closest town to the ruins, we boarded the first bus back to Palenque. As soon as the bus doors opened we ran to the jungle grove that we discovered the day before. The sun was just coming up and as we got closer we noticed that the rising sun shone directly onto one of the smaller temples. After consulting our map we discovered that this was the Temple of the Rising Sun.

We climbed the steep steps, and when we reached the top, the sun shone into the temple interior like a laser beam. The carved stone hieroglyphics reliefs depicting offerings to the sun came to life. Despite never having been in a Mayan temple, everything felt familiar. In the villages I felt grounded, centered and more in my body than I was used to. The ruins amplified these feelings.

This was a place of power and my body, mind and spirit soaked it in like a nurturing balm.

Daniel and I knelt on the stone floor, and except for the continuous chorus of birds, it was quiet and still. Wearing our handwoven wedding shirts and dripping with sweat, we looked at one another and began the ceremony. I held a single yellow flower that I picked on the way to the temple and timidly spoke my marriage vows. A wave of nervousness came over me and I read a poem I wrote and spontaneously blurt out vows that I am not sure made sense. Daniel spoke a bit more eloquently and promised his love and commitment. We then exchanged the silver rings that we had a local craftsman make a few weeks' prior. They each had a symbol of a snake carved into them to symbolize continuity and wisdom. We were married and quietly sat facing one another.

Several minutes later, the quiet spell was broken by the sound of approaching tourists. We took this as a signal that the ceremony was over. As we made our way down the steps, the sun having cast its spell on our ceremony was now high in the sky. Instead of friends or family greeting us, familiar spirit friends wove in and out of my awareness.

Dazed and walking in no particular direction we came upon the large ball court where the Mayans had played a game called Pitz. As I walked the length of the court, psychic energy radiated up and down my arms and legs in waves of tingling surges. I could see and feel the seriousness of the players and the intensity through which they played. Points were scored by bouncing a rubber ball a little bigger than a softball, which at times contained a human skull, into a net attached to the side of the court.

The game symbolized the transition and transformation of life and death. A large stone hieroglyphic at one end of the court described it as a portal into another world. However, the game was more than metaphoric. At its conclusion there was often a human sacrifice, usually a beheading. Many Mayan scholars believe that it was the winner, not the loser, that was chosen for this honor.

On one side of the ball court was a massive two-level structure that overlooked the pyramids and temples. The second floor was a large flat rock from which you could see the thick green jungle spread out for miles. In one corner there was a large raised flat stone that caught the attention of my psychic radar. It seemed to vibrate and I was surprised when my information leaflet described it as the altar where animal and human sacrifices were carried out. I didn't intuitively feel fear or dread from the stone. Instead, the energy felt freeing and more like an opening or energy portal. Despite the loss of life that took place there, it emanated a transcendent quality similar to the ball court. Transfixed by the spirits and energy that seemed to vibrate from the stone altar, I was startled by a couple coming up the stairs. They were laughing about a funny hat that someone in their group was wearing and their conversation snapped me out of the otherworldly vibrations I was experiencing.

After visiting the remaining temples, palaces and pyramids and the spirits that still stood guard within them, we were hungry and tired. Back on the bus watching the palace pyramid fade from view, I looked down at the silver band around my finger. My heart was flip-flopping with feelings of joy, elation, vulnerability and stress all mixed together. Even though the ceremony was not presided over by a minister or another official, I was married, heart and soul. In a moment of doubt, I realized I didn't have a clue as to what it meant to be a wife and a psychic one at that. Being psychic and talking to spirits while single and on my own was one thing. However, being married and talking to spirits might pose some issues.

Early on in our relationship I shared the psychic phenomena that I had experienced over the years with Daniel. However, I didn't go into great detail and describe the play-by-play continuous stream of intuitive awareness that flowed through me. The fear that I was too odd and that maybe there was something wrong with me nipped at my heels. It followed me around and teased me with threats of future embarrassment and abandonment. Wanting to do all that I could to devote myself to the relationship, I naively thought and hoped that the psychic stuff might just fade away.

If there was such a thing as normal, I wanted to experience it. As the bus pulled to our stop, visions of what it would be like to be part of a family with a home, and doing all the things that I imagined other people did, paraded through my mind. In my heart I knew that the idea that there was a normal life was just an illusion. However, I still held onto it.

To celebrate our wedding we found an open grill restaurant for dinner and sat outdoors on the terrace. The sun was setting and a mariachi band played lively and typical Mexican music. My chicken was dry and tough and my bottled beer was a bit warm, and it all felt perfect.

Part VII Many More Psychic Miles

Chapter 29

Empathic Stress

As the plane's wheels touched down on the runway, my stomach churned with stress. I was not in a hurry to collect my things and disembark. I hadn't been back in my hometown for several years, and I was excited and yet dreaded seeing my family. After sending a letter to my mother letting her know that I was married, she extended what felt like a sincere desire to see me and meet Daniel. Still, I was nervous and didn't know what to expect. The last time I saw my mother she had accused me of being a drug addict who needed tough love. Although I didn't do drugs and only had a beer or wine now and then, she told me that I had to get straight before she would have anything to do with me. Nothing I said would convince her that I did not have a drug problem. The pain of this accusation was still present. Although it was covered over with more confidence, independence and the love of a partner, it still hurt.

Despite our unresolved and wounded past, my arrival was calm and non-eventful. My mother and two brothers met us at the door. After a long silent look from my mother, we shared a stiff hug.

For the most part my mother looked the same as when I left, but her behavior was eerily different. Taped to the refrigerator, the bathroom mirror and the kitchen cabinets were index cards with handwritten positive statements, like, *Live, Laugh, Love* and *God Loves You*. We didn't talk about the past and it appeared as if all was forgotten. There were no questions asking where I had been or what had I been doing for the past several years. Instead my mother told me about her church, Bible study and prayer groups. Having been trained and ordained as a home missionary with the Methodist church, she had taken on more leadership roles in her congregation.

As an expression of Christian charity and to supplement my mother's income, two women from the state mental hospital were now living in my old bedroom. During the push to deinstitutionalize many of the long-term residents in the state mental hospital, my mother became an in-home care provider. The two women who shared my room had lived their entire lives in a state hospital. Like others who have been institutionalized for a long period of time, they were good at following directions and staying in their room for long periods of time. My mother was the person in charge and they did what they were told, including daily chores and yard-work. Although their quirks and idiosyncrasies surfaced, my mother clearly had the upper hand.

For the duration of our visit we slept in the basement and read the *Daily Word*, a Methodist inspirational prayer book, before we politely ate dinner. The smoking, drinking, swearing, throwing things and constantly dating mother of my younger years was gone. When needed she was a master magician. Capable of momentous change, my mother had the ability to reinvent herself at will. Without too much thought, her personality, likes and dislikes, whoever she had been, could be cast aside like an out-of-style pair of shoes. She took on new interests and goals, and like a well-seasoned actress, played the part with ease and confidence.

All of this would have been fine and dandy had I not been empathic. As any emotional intuitive can attest to, there is a whole lot of truth in the form of feelings, sensations and thoughts simmering behind appearances. I acutely felt my mother's desire to be this new and improved person. I knew she tried and wanted to be the calm and devoted woman that she presented herself to be, yet she exuded an unsettled, almost hyper anxiety and stress. She was fearful that I might upend her carefully crafted new image and I made her nervous. Although she wanted me to visit, it was easier when I was not there. I understood her feelings and was glad that she was active and had friends and purpose. However, I mourned our emotional distance and I didn't trust her. Despite the truce, we were no closer.

Instead of allowing pent-up emotions to surface and share from the heart, our conversation included benign pleasantries such as: "Good morning, what are you going to do today?" or "When I get home, we can all have dinner together."

All the while my stomach clinched, I became tired, had headaches and spent a lot of time in the basement. It was cold, dark and safe there. When I was not able to go to the woods as a child, this is where I was able to feel the presence and listen to my sister and my other spirit friends. Now back in my childhood home after several years, the quiet cool basement didn't bring my spirit friends any closer. The thick layers of unspoken stress and confusion felt like heavy sludge and prevented any helpful conversation with my guides. Although I felt their presence, they were drowned out by the silent, but still loud minefield of emotions.

Chapter 30

The Spirits Warn of Fire

The visit home went as well as could be expected, and after a few weeks, we were ready to make our way back to California. Thanks to the financial wedding gifts that we received from Daniel's family, we had a little bit of money. We decided to buy a car and drive across country. After seeing several junky cars in our price range that looked like they wouldn't have made it out of the state without breaking down, we began to feel discouraged. Then one morning while checking out ads, I noticed a US postal truck for sale. We joked about how much fun it would be to drive it across country and decided to go have a look. After a test drive we bought it. Although the steering wheel was on the wrong side and it only had one seat, it seemed ideal. We built a platform in the back of the truck which also served as a bed with storage underneath, and thanks to a lack of seat belt requirements at that time, an old green wicker chair with a red cushion became the front passenger seat.

A few days before heading back to California I took a pregnancy test. When the little wand revealed the plus sign of pregnancy, I felt only happiness. Our lack of money, employment and housing didn't bother me. The last several years of trusting that I would be led, and my needs provided for, instilled within me the confidence that everything would work out.

To the silent good-by waves of my mother and brothers, we set off early one morning, glad to be back on the road. However, it didn't take long to find out that the mail truck had its limitations. While we had driven it in town, we had not tested it on the highway. We soon discovered that the mail truck's maximum speed was fifty-five miles an hour. Anything over this caused the truck to violently shake. We also didn't have air conditioning and in the summer heat this would have come in handy. On the upside, most toll booths waved us through without asking for money.

After several endless days of driving through cornfields, up and down mountains, through the dry desert and intense heat, we made it to Southern California. It was a cool evening, the moon was high in the sky and the scent of wildflowers and sage filled the air.

Daniel had relatives that owned most of a mountain outside of Escondido and they gave us permission to build on land once owned by his father. With the help of friends and family, we built a small cabin on a platform overlooking a vast canyon. We had no running water, electricity or a bathroom, and instead relied on an outhouse, an old water tank that we periodically filled from a well, a propane stove and a cooler that required a daily trip for ice.

Daniel went to work in town as a handyman and carpenter and soon after moving in, I gave birth to our son. With no radio, phone or television it was quiet on top of the mountain. During the days as the warm dry breeze drifted in through the windows carrying with it the scent of the sagebrush that was everywhere, I cared for my baby. In the evening rattlesnakes gathered and hissed on the warm rocks beneath the platform of our house. There were so many of them I was afraid to go to the outhouse once the sun went down.

The spirits of the desert were as warm and welcoming as the climate. Since my first trip to California I felt an affinity with the land and the spirits, and often saw flashes of them on the hills and near a dried-up riverbed. However, as I peacefully sat with my son looking out over the distant hills, my tranquility and communion with the spirits began to be interrupted by visions of wildfires. Images of intense flames spreading over the hills and smoke-filled air crowded my inner vision. Fear and stress traveled up my spine, and although I tried to dismiss the visions, I knew that I was being warned.

Chapter 31

Murder and the Spirit Mother

Since moving to California I kept in contact with my mother by mail. When I told her of my concern over wildfires and lack of water, she invited me to Georgia where she had taken a job as the assistant director of a Methodist children's home. Despite my reservations, I still felt a pull to be closer to her, and to try and mend the division that separated us. When Daniel was offered a job that came with a small house we decided to make the move.

After living in Southern California for a couple of years, the move to rural Georgia produced a bit of a culture shock. The children's home was located in a small town that was overgrown with thick kudzu and red soil, while the main street was mostly used-car lots and fast-food restaurants. Soon after being hired, my mother integrated the two separate Methodist orphanages located not far from one another. The big brick rather majestic-looking property was the white home. The smaller more run-down home was for black children. Many in the area did not take kindly to the white and blacks kids living together, and saw my mother as an outsider from the North who was interfering. One night a wooden cross with a threatening note attached to it signed by the Ku Klux Klan was left in her driveway. Soon after she left her position to go to Duke Divinity School.

In the midst of this chaos I gave birth to a baby girl at home with a midwife. The only hospital within miles still sedated birthing mothers with a saddle block and often used forceps for delivery. After a short labor my ten-pound little girl burst into the world.

Although rural Georgia was less than an ideal place to live, we had no choice but to stay and save money. Daniel was in charge of the maintenance of the campus and I volunteered to teach art classes. The residents were mostly adolescents who had been in foster homes and orphanages for most of their lives. In addition to offices, a gym and dining hall, there were six or seven houses on the campus and each one housed a group of about ten boys or girls in the same age range.

We lived in a small house at the edge of the campus. One afternoon from my front window I saw a thin girl with straight brown hair who looked to be about fourteen walk to the edge of the property. With her hands on her hips she looked down the road for a couple of minutes, then turned around and walked back up the hill toward the main campus. A few days later she did the same thing. As I sat holding my baby daughter, I watched her silently stare at the road and knew that she was contemplating running away. As I felt her feelings of sadness and confusion, I became aware of a woman spirit by her side. With a distressed look on her face, the spirit clutched her heart with her hands, and a sharp feeling of fear and dread suddenly came over me. The spirit, who I realized was her mother, seemed to be trying to influence her to turn around and not run away. A moment later the girl went back up the hill.

Later that day when I saw the woman who was in charge of the girls' group, I asked her, "Who is the pretty new girl?"

"Oh, that would be Lisa," she answered.

"How is she doing?"

"She's having a hard time adjusting. All this is new for her. Never been in a group home before. Her mom died and no relatives would take her in. We're trying to get her settled," she said.

"I've seen her walk to the edge of the property a few times," I said.

"Oh, I know, she talks about leaving all the time. Bless her heart. We'll just keep trying."

For the next several days, I watched for Lisa but she never came back.

About a week later on a trip to the mall in a neighboring town, Lisa disappeared. While walking in the crowd of shoppers, she just seemed to vanish. Her disappearance was reported to the police, but no one seemed too concerned. Like other runaways the staff at the home assumed she would turn up. However, at night I couldn't sleep and knew that something was wrong. One morning, I started to cry while thinking of her and attributed my intense emotions to postpartum depression. Still, I couldn't shake the alarming dread and sadness I felt when I thought of her. Watching the news a few weeks later there was a report that a female body had been found at the bottom of a ravine in the bordering town. I knew it was her. A day later we learned that the body had been identified as Lisa and that she had been tortured before being murdered. A man and woman were eventually arrested and charged. They too had been raised in foster homes and met her the night she went missing at the mall. They gave no reason for killing her.

Haunted with images of Lisa and the suffering that she endured at the end of her life, I wondered if there was anything that I could have done to save her from the cruel and painful death. Haunted by the image of her staring down the street with her mother's spirit by her side, I wondered if there was something more that I could have done. Although her mother's spirit didn't seem to notice me, I knew that she was concerned and worried, and yet powerless to help her daughter. Day after day in my thoughts I replayed the events that led up to her death and questioned what I could have done differently that might have prevented the tragic outcome. I was mad at myself and frustrated with being psychic and not doing more to help others.

Chapter 32

A Grandmother Spirit Welcomes Me Home

Once we managed to save a little money, Daniel and I knew it was time to move on. The small Georgia town had its charms, but openness to new ideas was not one of them. Being psychic was generally perceived as the Devil's work and I lived with the stress of being found out.

Opportunity pointed us in the direction of North Carolina. Our plan was to buy a house that we could renovate over time. Not far from where we were house-sitting there was an older home that caught my attention. Even though it was falling apart, it was more than we could afford. We decided to take a look at it anyway, and as soon as I went in I was startled by the warm presence of a spirit. I immediately recognized her as my grandmother, not through family, but my spiritual grandmother. Even though I had not previously been aware of her, it felt as if I had always known her.

"This is your home and where you are meant to be," she whispered to me.

There was a warmth and love that flowed from this message that I couldn't resist. The next day we submitted an offer. Upset with our low bid, the owners didn't take our offer seriously. After several days of not hearing back, we assumed there was no deal. Confused by the message that I had received from the spirit grandmother, I reached out to her. Almost immediately I felt her warmth and assurance that everything would work out.

About a month after we submitted our offer, we received a phone call from one of the owners of the house. She said that her husband wanted more for the house, but they needed to sell it as soon as possible. She accepted our price and eventually persuaded her husband to do the same.

Even through the sky peeked through the holes in the roof, there was no heat, and the plumbing was full of leaks, the house was ours. Little by little we did what we could do to repair and renovate it.

In the backyard there was a shed that we converted into an art studio where I wove and painted silk. To make a little money I sold the scarves, placemats and other items that I created in shops and craft fairs. I also began to teach weaving and other craft and fiber classes at the local arts council. One morning while in my studio contemplating my next project, I saw a clear image of a unique-looking woven and silk painted jacket. I had never seen anything like this and didn't know if it was actually possible to make it. However, a rush of inspiration motivated me to give it a try. As I wove, cut and sewed, the jacket seemed to have a mind of its own and wanted to come to life. When it was completed, I was pleasantly surprised.

Using my psychic ability to create opened up new possibilities. Excited, I pressed on and continued to use my intuition to guide the direction of my work. Others also responded in positive ways and more galleries sought me out and sales increased. In my little studio I was as happy as I had ever been. So it was a surprise when uncomfortable past memories and emotions began to spontaneously surface. I tried to shoo these feelings away and get back to being stress free. However, this only seemed to make the past pain hold on tighter.

Ever close, my native American guide Tetchuwatchu whispered in my ear that it was time to allow the stuffed-away unresolved feelings of my past to surface and be released. I tried to ignore him and the uncomfortable feelings, but I couldn't keep either at bay. The buried away grief of my father's absence and my confusion and pain over the emotional distance between my mother and I came rolling in like high tide during a full moon. Some of the memories and feelings were relentless, and at times felt overwhelming. One night I woke sweating and anxious with the odd sensation that someone or something was pressing pressure points in my back. Three spirits who I didn't recognize came forward and told me that they wanted to help me to release the blocked energy. Part of me wanted to resist, but it felt so good. I could feel the stress and pain let go and eventually fell back to sleep. In the morning I woke up refreshed and felt better than I had in a long time. I was grateful for their intervention. However, my guides told me that I needed to do more. They gently suggested I also get more worldly help through this process.

After a few referrals, I settled into talk therapy with a kind older man who looked as if he had just gotten out of bed. His clothing was disheveled and his dimly-lit office had piles of magazines and stacks of paper scattered throughout the room. An old slanted picture of a ship at sea hung on the wall. He seemed relaxed about the whole business of therapy, and when I talked he often seemed to fall asleep. Which was fine with me, it actually made it a little easier. But it wasn't easy. One day he casually said something about my being abused as a child and I was taken aback. He seemed to think that I knew that I had been physically and emotionally abused. I didn't, and at the same time it was obvious and made perfect sense. The fighter and survivor in me didn't want to believe that this was true. Almost as if any admission of weakness and the whole facade of my invincibility would fall away. However, the cat was out of the bag and eventually I came to accept that I was damaged goods.

Surprisingly, this admission had the opposite effect of what I feared might happen. Instead of falling apart, I felt stronger and more confident. My heart opened little by little, and I was better able to feel and accept the love of my spirit friends and my family.

Although Mary's healing energy had done a good job at uncovering old wounds and filling me with love, there was still stuck pain in my body. Pain clouds everything. It acts as a barrier to receiving higher vibrations, and this is what I wanted. More than anything I yearned for the uplifting sensations and the warm flow of spiritual love to move through me. Being psychic was not my goal. I wanted to live in this love and I was willing to do whatever was needed to more fully be in this presence.

Chapter 33

Troubled Teens and Mother Mary

As I settled into a satisfying routine of family and work, I was surprised when my guides started to nudge me in another direction. One afternoon after feeling Tetchuwatchu close by all day, I asked him what he wanted.

"It's time, you are meant to be working with others," Tetchuwatchu whispered in my ear.

I was not too excited by this message. I wanted to focus on creating art and teaching a few classes now and then. I wasn't interested in pursuing another profession.

"Just let me weave a while longer. I'll work with others soon," I replied.

For a few days everything was quiet. Then again I felt his presence and heard the same message, and again I resisted. Eventually his suggestion to work with others became so persistent I began to wonder if I had a choice.

With Tetchuwatchu's determination and gift of persuasion, I wasn't too surprised when I bumped into my supervisor on my way to teach a class. He had a knack for putting the people and situations that would serve my current lesson or direction right in front of me.

"Would you be interested in more teaching?" she asked. Then before I could answer, she continued. "We need more teachers to go into the schools and work with some of the special needs classes. Come in tomorrow and we'll talk about it."

A few weeks later I found myself sitting next to a young male who had been diagnosed with severe autism. Unenthusiastically he pushed a hard lump of clay around on his desk. My guides encouraged me to wrap my hands arounds his and we made a small bowl together. A big grin spread across his face and he laughed wholeheartedly. For the remainder of the school year, I worked in the schools in the morning and wove in the afternoons. Although I enjoyed working with the special needs kids, I was restless. Something was off and knew that it was only a matter of time before it came my way.

Then one morning on my way to teach, I passed an old dilapidated school. Something about it caught my attention, and a tingle went up my spine and my heart pumped with excitement. I knew that this intuitive sign was significant, but I wasn't sure what it meant. After asking around I discovered that even though the school looked as if it might collapse at any moment, it was being used as part of the hospital school. Twenty to thirty teenagers who had been expelled from public school and arrested for violent crimes came here as an alternative to jail.

As one of the other art teachers described the dismal conditions of the school, I asked her, "Do they have an art program?"

In my heart I knew that I was meant to work with these students.

When I approached my supervisor at the arts council and asked her if I could run an art program at the school, she looked at me as if she couldn't quite understand what I said. Again, I expressed my desire to teach art there. This time she simply said, "No, it's too dangerous."

I was not ready to give up. I knew it was the right thing to do. The next time I approached my supervisor I asked her if I could meet and talk with the head of the school to get his input. She hesitated and told me that she had to think about it.

The next week I went ahead and set up a meeting with him. A large middle-aged man who I liked from the start, he took the time to listen thoughtfully to my proposal. When I was done he thanked me for coming in, but didn't think that the students would be interested.

"Why don't you come back at the end of the week, and talk to the students. If any are interested, we'll go from there," he said.

A few days later, all eyes were on me as I walked into a class of five adolescent males. Not allowed to talk or interact, they sat at their desks with worksheets and a pencil. The ceiling in the shabby and stuffy room had a large water stain with crumbling tile and insulation hanging out of it. The desks, too small for the long-legged boys, were covered with gang signs. A tall man in the front of the room stood up from behind another small desk and introduced me to the students. Leaning against the back wall were three large men who stood guard and didn't crack a smile.

"Is anyone interested in doing some art?" I asked.

I described a few of the things that we would do, but there was no response, just more intimidating stares. A few awkward moments later, I said, "If anyone changes their mind, let me know. It might be fun."

As I put my hand on the door to leave, I heard a lone voice say, "Okay, I'll do art."

After repeating my request in the two other classes, I received a few more positive responses.

When I told my supervisor that I had met with the director of the program, she was not happy. However, when they offered the arts council a generous budget for my services, she agreed to let me give it a try.

Deeper than our Skin

Twice a week I went to the school and worked with the one or two kids in each class that were interested. Although they were suspicious of me, others slowly joined in one at a time. Gaining their trust didn't come easy and after several months they still found new ways to test me.

Tequan was a particularly difficult fifteen year old who looked as if he could have been in his twenties. One day in the hallway I happened to catch a glimpse of a thicker-built man in spirit following behind him. I knew that this was Tequan's grandfather and that he was trying to help him. A short time later, Tequan sat close to me in class, and made continual and subtle threatening remarks. As he continued to spout veiled threats, I made a plea to his grandfather.

Almost immediately I felt an emotional wave of the loss and grief that Tequan continually experienced. His mother had abandoned him when he was young, and his anger and pain over this was destroying him. The emotional intensity touched my heart and I could feel how much he was hurting. For a magical moment, I felt the kind of love that a mother has for a child. I imagined cradling him as a baby and being delighted with his little toes and fingers. I could feel Mother Mary's spirit and I knew that this was the kind of love that I needed to feel toward him.

Tequan continued to stare at me with angry eyes and I asked him, "Why do you want to intimidate me?"

This of course bolstered his ego and he laughed. "Oh, Ms. Dillard, you scared?" he asked.

"A little bit, but I don't think you really want to hurt me," I said.

Again, he laughed and said, "How you know that? Could be I do... you know what I'm sayin'?"

I looked at him with his balled fists and glazed-over eyes, and said, "There's nothing you can say that's going to make me stop caring about you. I know you're hurting. I've been hurt too and I know how it feels."

Still angry, Tequan looked at me, but said nothing. For the remainder of the class he stared out the window. In our next class he was quiet and toward the end of class started to engage in the project that everyone else was working on. From then on he became one of my strongest allies. Never again did he taunt me or be disrespectful. When new students came into the school and began to harass me, he intervened.

"Come on, she a'right," he'd say, and they would leave me alone.

After summer break the school moved to a different location

to accommodate more students and I went with them. Within a few months, the art program took off. I was teaching several classes a day and all the students were involved. By mid-year the school provided another budget increase and wanted to expand the program.

My arts council supervisor was resistant. However, after discussion, meetings and intervention with higher-ups, the program was a go and I was able to hire a few more art instructors.

Mainstream teachers and school system administrators came in to observe as the art class was the only program that the students willingly participated in. When I was asked what contributed to the success of the program, I talked about things like how I encouraged self-expression and the open and accepting environment. What I didn't mention was the role that intuition and communicating with the students' loved ones on the other side and other spirits played.

Connecting to the students through this more soulful approach may have been what motivated one of the younger students to question my race. Abused as a child, Jay still had scars on his arms and legs where he was burnt with cigarettes from his mother's boyfriend. In the cold of winter he often came to school wearing just a tee shirt and no jacket. He lived in a group home with several of the other boys where he had a difficult time fitting in. Jay took to following me around the school and we became friends.

One morning as I entered his classroom, I noticed him intently staring at me.

"Mz. Dillard, you black?" he asked.

"What?" I said.

He seemed unable to take his eyes off of me and asked, again, "You black?"

"Jay, I am about as white as you can get," I said. "I have red hair, green eyes and very white skin."

This only seemed to confuse him and he continued to

quizzically look at me.

I mentioned this to another teacher, a black woman, and she told me that Jay had stopped her and asked her the same question.

There was nothing wrong with Jay's eyesight or his intelligence. The next time I saw him he smiled at me and called me his "green-eyed black sister."

Give More When Empty

Although there were surprising and unexpected positive and transformative encounters, the school was still a difficult environment. The students were predominately adolescent males, who had been in and out of foster and group homes, experienced violence and had been arrested for various crimes. We used to joke that our alumni news could be found in the newspaper crime report column.

The energy of the school was often angry and thick with the threat of violence. An outburst, fight or attack could happen at any time. Some days just going to the school was exhausting and I started to experience panic attacks. While driving, shopping or at home with my children, my throat would suddenly tighten up. I would have a hard time breathing, and stress and anxiety would shoot up my spine.

The therapy and other healing work I was involved in was not much help, and any relief was only temporary. One afternoon I sat in meditation on a small cushion in the corner of my art studio. Thoughts raced through my mind and waves of stress flowed unabated through my body. When I asked my guides how to lessen the stressful impact that the school was having on me, a soft blue light streamed into my awareness and I knew that Mary was close. In a soft whisper I heard, "Love them."

"I do love them," I replied.

"Love them and open your heart," I heard again and then again.

In my characteristic self-centered way, I protested. "What do you mean? How can I love them more? What about me? Who's going to love and help me?"

A gentle warmth filled me, but I was still a bit frustrated. It felt as if I needed love and support, and I was being asked to give even more. I didn't know if I had anything left.

The following week at the school, I attempted to open my heart and express more love. Yet, I still felt a high degree of stress and anxiety. This continued throughout the week. Then on Friday afternoon as I was leaving, I noticed the students playing basketball. My car was parked near the court and I went over and leaned on the chain-link fence and watched them. I suddenly became dizzy and slipped into a light altered state. Without intent or effort a swelling wave of love filled me. Tingling energy moved up my spine and I felt this warm love energy flow to the sweaty and swearing boys playing basketball. For several minutes I stood transfixed in the warm sun while love moved through me to them. As the boys continued to play I became aware of light and energy dancing around them, and the hardened tension and stress that I had been experiencing melted away. From then on feelings of stress and panic were never again an issue.

Chapter 34

Psychic Lessons

I thought that creating an art therapy program for troubled teenagers would quiet the constant inner message being broadcast to me from my spirit guides. I was wrong.

They still whispered, "It's time to work with others."

To which I replied, "I am helping others."

Although I played dumb to what my guides were referring to, I knew exactly what they meant. I had skirted the obvious for a long time. My intuition and psychic abilities were only getting stronger. Yet, despite the constant nudging from the spirit realm, I had no interest in sharing my psychic impressions with others.

Even though I loved being able to feel the presence of my guides and communicate with them, I wondered if being a professional psychic and medium was even helpful. Feeding the hungry, providing clean water to indigenous villages and helping teens to heal were all valid forms of service. I wasn't sure that giving psychic readings was truly useful.

Just the thought of being a psychic didn't sit well with me and I was a little embarrassed by the idea. Psychics, it seemed to me, set themselves apart from others. They viewed themselves as special and believed that they had insights and gifts that others did not. Although I saw spirits and talked to them, it was natural and there didn't seem to be anything special about it.

Between work at the school and being a mother, I had little time to spare. My family was my main focus and I wanted to give them what I considered a normal life. My idealized vision of family life didn't include psychic awareness, seeing spirits, going from one place to another and having no home.

I was also reluctant to put myself out in the community as a psychic and medium. I didn't want to be judged and viewed as a fraud or delusional. In the conservative part of the country where I lived Baptist and Evangelical Christian churches were popular and the prevailing view was that anything paranormal was evil. This was not the kind of challenge I wanted to take on. Working in my studio, spending time with my children and husband, and developing a career as an artist and teacher made more sense. I dug my heels in and ignored my guides' whispers to take my psychic gifts to another level.

"Just let me be for a while. I'm not ready," I told my guides.

Psychic Information Highways

However, the spirit realm had their own agenda. As I had already learned, spirit guides are not here to do our bidding. Despite my reluctance, they continued to teach and prepare me to give readings to others.

One morning as I sat and weaved I saw an image of my Native American guide, dressed like a rodeo clown and riding a horse. With a silly look on his face, he paraded across my inner vision jumping off of cliffs and doing cartwheels.

"What are you doing?" I asked him.

No answer, just another image of him on a horse flying up in the air like an acrobat. He kept up these antics until I couldn't help but stop what I was doing and laugh. However, this was more than just an entertaining sideshow.

Along with the images I heard the message, "Pay attention, I'm going to show you how it works."

I didn't know what he was talking about, but he had my attention. Intrigued, I quietly waited. Suddenly I was out of my body and floating alongside him. Suspended in the air, I felt a buzzing current of energy all around me.

"Psychic energy information flows along electromagnetic currents," Tetchuwatchu said.

I then felt and saw different currents of energy, some intense and others more subdued, crisscrossing around me. They reminded me of a series of highways, bridges and overpasses all intertwined together, yet flowing smoothly.

"You can tap into these currents or frequencies. It is like changing the stations on a radio," he said.

A stronger wave of energy moved by me and I became aware of a portal-like opening leading into it.

"When you feel drawn to one of the currents, let go into it, open your consciousness and feel and see what comes to you," he said.

Although I wasn't sure how to do what Tetchuwatchu instructed, I did my best and was surprised that this seemed to work. Once I felt the subtle buzzing of the psychic current, I allowed myself to drift into it. Immediately I saw images of spirits on the other side. It looked as if they were lining up and preparing to communicate to their loved ones still in the physical realm. I realized that higher more evolved souls were guiding them on how to better connect with and positively influence those in the physical world. Soon another current of energy came close, and as these images faded, I effortlessly flowed into this different frequency. Here I felt the longing and loneliness of people still in the physical world. Then in an image I saw a woman mourning the loss of her son. She was reaching out to him, and at the same time, he was standing next to her with his hand on her shoulder. Confused and crying, she didn't know that he was close. As quickly as I had entered this current, I moved out of it and heard Tetchuwatchu say, "The currents will also respond to your requests. Try it. Ask a question and feel how the energy around you changes and responds."

Curious, I asked about one of the teenagers that I had been working with. Resistant to any kind of connection, I wondered how to help him begin to heal.

"Once you have your question, make it concise and project it into the energy surrounding you. Then feel for the current or frequency that responds by coming close with a buzzing or the subtle feeling of a higher intensity."

After projecting my question, I paused and waited. A vibrating wave of energy drifted by me and I imagined my consciousness flowing into it. As I did this I was surprised by how dynamic it felt. Suddenly I saw an image of my student and felt his fear. He thought he lacked intelligence and was afraid that if he spoke up he would be teased or embarrass himself. Next to him was a woman spirit who felt like his grandmother. She encouraged me to keep working with him as she felt that he was coming around. The energy then dissipated and Tetchuwatchu was gone.

For the next several weeks Tetchuwatchu returned, and we continued to practice sensing, communicating and tuning into different frequencies of energy. It was stimulating and I enjoyed the sensation of merging my consciousness with energy in this way.

The Elder

Early one morning on a day off from teaching, I sat at my loom trying to focus on the pattern and colors I was working with. Unexpectedly a wave of dizziness came over me and I felt fatigued. I put my weaving shuttle down and went and sat in an old overstuffed chair. Immediately, I felt pulled within. When I closed my eyes I became aware of a guide that I had previously seen and felt a few times. However, his presence was much stronger and clearer than it had been in the past. He was thin, with dark eyes and wore a beige-looking sari. White and gold glowing energy emanated from him.

"I'm the Elder," he said.

He looked at me with penetrating eyes and I felt completely seen and known. His gaze felt electrifying and at the same time peaceful. Then he was gone.

Feeling reenergized I went back to weaving.

Intrigued by the Elder, I wondered if he would be back. A few days later after a similar feeling of tired dizziness, I again saw and felt him. However, his energy was powerful and I could only stay connected to him for short periods of time. When I asked him why he seemed elusive, he told me that I needed to raise and maintain a higher energy vibration.

"How do I do this?" I asked.

"We are working on helping you," he said.

I wasn't sure how the spirits were helping me, but I was slowly able to be in his presence for longer periods of time.

One afternoon during one of my meditation sessions I felt the familiar jolt of the Elder's presence. Unlike some of my guides, he wasn't warm and fuzzy. Instead he spoke in a straightforward, yet kind manner.

"Are you ready to help others through this work?" he asked.

"No," I mumbled.

"Perhaps I can help you to enjoy the process more. It can feel good. Are you willing to allow me to share space with you?"

I didn't know what this meant, but thought it couldn't be any weirder than what was already happening.

I agreed, and after a momentary pause, a flow of warm and tingling energy moved up my spine. My muscles relaxed and I was more aware of my body. I started to stretch, and sat up straight. I was alert and it felt like I was buzzing with positivity.

"Doesn't this feel better?" the Elder asked.

However, his voice came from within me and I realized that his spirit was inside my physical body. As the Elder moved through me I felt vibrant, positive and loving. His energy opened my heart and all of my senses were enhanced. At the same time I became acutely aware of my feelings of low self-esteem, and I realized that my hesitancy to embrace my psychic awareness was rooted in fear and the desire to hide. The Elder's presence was powerful and it seemed to stir up and magnify my emotional blocks and resistance, and heal. Feeling uplifted and peaceful, I wanted to stay in his energy for as long as I could. However, a few minutes later I became tired and sleepy. As he faded out of my awareness, he told me to have a recorder ready for our next session.

A few days later I sat on a pillow on the floor of my studio and tried to meditate. As I focused on my breath, my mind kept wandering to the Elder. Although at the time it felt oddly natural and relaxing to share my physical space with him, I began to feel nervous and overwhelmed. I couldn't fully understand what was happening with him and why. As feelings of resistance surfaced, I remembered the pledge that I made to allow a higher spiritual presence to use and direct me. The spirit realm had always been there when I needed support, comfort, love and guidance. Although my spirit guides often frustrated, confused or led me into situations that I would have liked to avoid, they never let me down. They were my safety net and my rock.

My therapist once asked me who was there for me when I was younger.

"Some have a grandparent or another relative, neighbor or teacher, that they turn to in difficult times," he said.

"There was no one," I said.

However, this was not entirely true. I could always rely on my spirit guides and friends.

Although I was hesitant and didn't know what was happening with the Elder and what the outcome would be, I knew in my heart I could trust him.

The next afternoon with my tape recorder next to me, I closed my eyes and felt the Elder's energy move up my spine. I adjusted my posture and sat straight as his expansive energy released pent-up tension. Suddenly, I heard myself talk, only it wasn't my voice. It was a deeper male voice with an odd accent that I couldn't identify. I had a hard time pronouncing words and could feel myself struggling to communicate.

Realizing that this is why I had the tape recorder, I turned it on. Despite the strange sensations and oddity of the situation, his presence felt delightful. He spoke in a light and crisp kind of way, and I both spoke and listened to him. Once again, I felt a wave of tiredness and he was gone.

A few days later I was back at it. The amount of time that I could hold the Elder's energy was increasing. Every session had an agenda and teaching. In one session in response to my questioning if being psychic could really help others, he said:

"Being psychic is simply allowing more of your true self to be part of your physical experience. You are not just blood and bones and a thinking brain. The illusion of the physical world is that it is physical. This is quite funny from our perspective. It is like putting on a Halloween costume and forgetting that you are really the person that chose the costume and put it on. When you listen to and develop psychic abilities you activate your spirit and energy body. Underneath that earth costume you're wearing you're an awful like us in the spirit world. You have capabilities that allow you to tap into the source of all wisdom and love. Being psychic is a practical way to be in this world. Intuition or psychic ability, whatever you prefer to call it, can be of valuable assistance in every problem, situation or predicament that life brings your way. We want you to experience joy, abundance, health and love. This is true reality and we want you to help others to experience this also."

Psychic Guidelines

One afternoon after settling into a meditative state, the Elder came forward and told me that there were a few guidelines I needed to adhere to as a psychic and medium. As usual I wasn't sure what he was referring to but I listened.

"Never interfere with another's free will and choice," he said. "Communicate as clearly as possible whatever you intuitively receive. Don't attempt to persuade others to follow a certain path or act in a specific way. Be compassionate and never shame another for their choices and actions. Let go of outcomes. If you interfere with another's karma you will become weighed down and overly burdened. Eventually your intuition will shut down.

Fear surfaces in many forms. It may appear as resistance, confusion, the need to be right and in a variety of other ways. It has no place in this work. If you feel fear within yourself or another, greet it with love and compassion.

The ego is the biggest deterrent and the root of intuitive doubt and inaccuracy. It too shows up in many disguises. Sometimes people will praise you and sometimes they will not like what you say. What others think is not important. It is tempting to want positive feedback and to be told that the information that you provide is correct. Sometimes this is useful, but not always. Instead care more about what God feels about what you communicate. Everything else is transitory and can become an obstacle. The ego will always want to take control. If you let it, you will lose your way and become exhausted.

You have been taught to access high levels of energy and you know how to tap into divine guidance. Don't think of yourself as one person doing this on your own. Never separate yourself from the spirit energy that you are part of. Flow into all forms and let them flow into you. This is how you help others to heal and move into their full potential. We are always with you working through you."

I didn't understand everything that he said, but knew that in time it would make more sense.

After a few months of working with the Elder, he announced that he was ready to do readings. I laughed at this and wondered how he was going to go about it. I certainly wasn't about to tell anyone what was going on.

A few days later I was talking to a friend, and although I had no intention of sharing what was happening with the Elder, I did. She seemed excited and wanted a reading with him. With her encouragement I sat down on the floor in her bedroom, the Elder didn't like sitting in a chair, and let him talk. They were both delighted. The Elder loved people and was beaming with positivity. My friend told a few friends of hers about the reading and they too asked for sessions. They in turn told others and soon I was giving readings on a regular basis. After a few months the Elder told me that it was time for him to fade into the background and for me to take over.

"I will always be with you, working through you. There are many others who are a part of our work. They too love you and want to help and give to others," he said.

After this his energy began to fade. Just as he had said, I still felt his presence, supporting me as I took over the readings.

After several months of communicating with the other side and sharing the energy information that I received to others, I woke up one morning and didn't want to do it anymore. It was this simple for me. I was done and I had no interest in being psychic or talking to the other side. It felt as if my life was being taken from me and I wanted it back. Still teaching and doing art, I was exhausted by trying to keep up with the demands. I knew my spirit guides and friends wouldn't understand so I stopped meditating and did my best not to listen to them. I hung up a metaphoric sign that said, "Closed," and walked away.

However, shutting off my intuition came with side effects that I didn't expect. Although I was partially successful at keeping the spirit realm at bay, I was miserable. At night I tossed and turned and developed insomnia. I was tired most of the time and my creativity took a nosedive. Although I felt like a wandering ghost with no direction, my stubbornness wouldn't let me give in.

About two months after going on my psychic strike I drove down a lightly traveled road on a beautiful blue-sky sunny day. Suddenly my car was struck at the driver's side by someone who had run a red light. The impact spun my car around in a series of full circles. As I watched my front fender fly into the air in a spectacular display of shiny light-filled loops and turns, I felt Tetchuwatchu by my shoulder.

This was no accident, I realized. The spirits wanted my attention.

Without further discussion, bargaining or fear, I said out loud, "Okay, I get it. I'm a psychic, thanks a lot."

Tetchuwatchu said nothing. When my car finally stopped its hissing gymnastic exhibition, it came to a stop and the side view mirror fell off. I could barely open the door and the next thing I knew I was being put on a stretcher and riding in an ambulance. As the driver and attendant chatted, I began to panic. Not because I was hurt; I knew I would be fine. What caused me more terror was my future. There was a bigger plan than mine that I was part of. There would be no more resistance and stubbornness.

The car accident left me with no serious injuries, but just enough damage in my neck and back to end weaving as a profession. Two weeks after the accident, I started giving readings full-time.

Chapter 35

Epilogue

My running was over. The years spent looking into the eyes of the suffering, staring down an empty highway and seeing and talking to spirits led me to deeper surrender. My vulnerabilities, pain and wandering had become my strength. Something divine, and yet vague, chased and finally caught me. It had been hiding within my pain, confusion and even within my resistance, and had always been with me. When that little wisp of breath left my lungs as a baby, I found what I was looking for. I had been going backwards all along in search of the love that returned me to this world with a little bit of heaven lodged in my soul.

For over thirty years, I lived in the house where once you could see the sky through the holes in the roof. It got patched up along with the rest of the house.

My mother died in 2001 from cancer. Although we never had a close relationship, she called me close to death one night.

"I was a lousy mother," she said. "Can you forgive me?"

With no hesitation, I did. St. Therese came to me a few hours after her death and took me to my mother in the spirit realm. She looked vulnerable and meek in a way that I had never seen her in the physical world. It was a gift to be able to say good-by to her.

A few years later, my father died. Although I tried to reconcile with him a few times, it never stuck. He had a new family and never showed much interest in reconnecting. Neither my sister nor I was mentioned in his obituary.

I lost touch with Bob, my step-adopted father. Thirty-five years after no contact, I searched his name on the Internet and found his obituary. Surprisingly I was listed as one of his daughters.

Daniel and I divorced after eighteen years of marriage. Toward the end of our relationship we went to marriage counseling. In the midst of a tense session he looked at our marriage counselor with wide-open eyes and exclaimed, "She talks to dead people!"

I guess he did have a problem with me being psychic after all. Soon after our divorce, our marriage counselor came to my office and asked me to communicate with her mother and father on the other side.

During the many years that I have talked to those on the other side and the spirits, and given readings to the lost, lonely, sick, suffering and grief-stricken, I have done my best to express compassion and share the love that I have received.

Over the years, I have come to see myself simply as a sieve. Full of empty spaces and cracks where the light seeps through.

ALL THINGS PARANORMAL

Investigations, explanations and deliberations on the paranormal, supernatural, explainable or unexplainable. 6th Books seeks to give answers while nourishing the soul: whether making use of the scientific model or anecdotal and fun, but always beautifully written.

Titles cover everything within parapsychology: how to, lifestyles, alternative medicine, beliefs, myths and theories.

If you have enjoyed this book, why not tell other readers by posting a review on your preferred book site?

Recent bestsellers from 6th Books are:

The Afterlife Unveiled
What the Dead Are Telling us About Their World!
Stafford Betty
What happens after we die? Spirits speaking through mediums
know, and they want us to know. This book unveils their world...
Paperback: 978-1-84694-496-3 ebook: 978-1-84694-926-5

Spirit Release
Sue Allen
A guide to psychic attack, curses, witchcraft, spirit attachment,
possession, soul retrieval, haunting, deliverance, exorcism and
more, as taught at the College of Psychic Studies.
Paperback: 978-1-84694-033-0 ebook: 978-1-84694-651-6

I'm Still With You
True Stories of Healing Grief Through Spirit Communication
Carole J. Obley
A series of after-death spirit communications which uplift, comfort
and heal, and show how love helps us grieve.
Paperback: 978-1-84694-107-8 ebook: 978-1-84694-639-4

Less Incomplete
A Guide to Experiencing the Human Condition Beyond the
Physical Body
Sandie Gustus
Based on 40 years of scientific research, this book is a dynamic
guide to understanding life beyond the physical body.
Paperback: 978-1-84694-351-5 ebook: 978-1-84694-892-3

Advanced Psychic Development
Becky Walsh
Learn how to practise as a professional, contemporary spiritual medium.
Paperback: 978-1-84694-062-0 ebook: 978-1-78099-941-8

Astral Projection Made Easy
Overcoming the Fear of Death
Stephanie June Sorrell
From the popular Made Easy series, *Astral Projection Made Easy* helps to eliminate the fear of death, through discussion of life beyond the physical body.
Paperback: 978-1-84694-611-0 ebook: 978-1-78099-225-9

The Miracle Workers Handbook
Seven Levels of Power and Manifestation of the Virgin Mary
Sherrie Dillard
Learn how to invoke the Virgin Mary's presence, communicate with her, receive her grace and miracles and become a miracle worker.
Paperback: 978-1-84694-920-3 ebook: 978-1-84694-921-0

Divine Guidance
The Answers You Need to Make Miracles
Stephanie J. King
Ask any question and the answer will be presented, like a direct line to higher realms... *Divine Guidance* helps you to regain control over your own journey through life.
Paperback: 978-1-78099-794-0 ebook: 978-1-78099-793-3

Beyond Photography
Encounters with Orbs, Angels and Mysterious Light Forms!
John Pickering, Katie Hall
Orbs have been appearing all over the world in recent years. This is the personal account of one couple's experience of this new phenomenon.
Paperback: 978-1-90504-790-1

Blissfully Dead
Life Lessons from the Other Side
Melita Harvey
The spirit of Janelle, a former actress, takes the reader on a fascinating and insightful journey from the mind to the heart.
Paperback: 978-1-78535-078-8 ebook: 978-1-78535-079-5

Does It Rain in Other Dimensions?
A True Story of Alien Encounters
Mike Oram
We have neighbors in the universe. This book describes one man's experience of communicating with other-dimensional and extra-terrestrial beings over a 50-year period.
Paperback: 978-1-84694-054-5

Electronic Voices: Contact with Another Dimension?
Anabela Mourato Cardoso
Career diplomat and experimenter Dr Anabela Cardoso covers the latest research into Instrumental Transcommunication and Electronic Voice Phenomena.
Paperback: 978-1-84694-363-8

The Hidden Secrets of a Modern Seer
Cher Chevalier
An account of near death experiences, psychic battles between
good and evil, multidimensional experiences and Demons and
Angelic Helpers.
Paperback: 978-1-84694-307-2 ebook: 978-1-78099-058-3

Readers of ebooks can buy or view any of these bestsellers by
clicking on the live link in the title. Most titles are published
in paperback and as an ebook. Paperbacks are available in
traditional bookshops. Both print and ebook formats are available
online.
Find more titles and sign up to our readers' newsletter at
http://www.johnhuntpublishing.com/mind-body-spirit.
Follow us on Facebook at https://www.facebook.com/OBooks
and Twitter at https://twitter.com/obooks.